Lean on God's Understanding

How to have a stress-free life

Ashley ✝ Lee

Cornerstone House

Cover design by Carley Lee
Book Layout ©2016 BookDesignTemplates.com

Lean on God's understanding: how to live a stress-free life / Ashley T Lee

ISBN: 978-0-578-63957-4

Lean on God's Understanding

How to have a stress-free life

Ashley T Lee

Contents

Dedicated to Eva, my grandmother, for being an inspirational example of a Christian woman,

To Becky, Betty, Fran, and Carolyn for their Christian influences and prayers as spiritual moms,

To my daughters, Carley and Christie, for their contributions to this book,

And finally, to Jesus Christ, my true inspiration and Savior.

Preface

Hebrews 1:1-4 (NKJV)
"God, who at various times and in various ways spoke
in time past to the fathers by the prophets,
has in these last days spoken to us by His Son,
whom He has appointed heir of all things,
through whom also He made the world;
who being the brightness of His glory
and the express image of His person,
and upholding all things by the word of His power,
when He had by Himself purged our sins,
sat down at the right hand of the Majesty
on high, having become so much better
than the angels, as He has by inheritance
obtained a more excellent name than they."

Hebrews 1 sums up the promises of God for us. Not the promises of some extravagant, lavish life on earth, but inheritance through the Savior of the world, Jesus Christ. Jesus is God's provision for our promise of hope, and my prayer is that you take hold of it through your adventure in this book.

Through years of pain and toil, God has taught me to "lean on God's understanding" and avoid the stress of living in the world. Avoiding stress might seem impossible, but note that in Mark 9:23, Jesus said, "If you can believe, all things are possible to him who believes."

Embark on the following 18 chapters to discover the glorious promises that God has in store for you while you wait on earth for the new heaven and new earth to be delivered.

7

Revelation 21:1-4 (NKJV)
"Now I saw a new heaven and a new earth,
for the first heaven and the first earth
had passed away. . . .
Then I, John, saw the holy city,
New Jerusalem, coming down out of heaven from God,
prepared as a bride adorned for her husband.
And I heard a loud voice from heaven saying,
"Behold, the tabernacle of God is with men,
and He will dwell with them,
and they shall be His people.
God Himself will be with them
and be their God. And God will
wipe away every tear from their eyes;
there shall be no more death,
nor sorrow, nor crying. There shall be no more pain,
for the former things have passed away."

CHAPTER 1

Stress Dilemma

Proverbs 3:5-6
"Trust in the Lord with all your heart
And do not lean on your own understanding.
In all your ways acknowledge Him,
And He will make your paths straight."

When a disruption happens in your life, stress is a normal reaction—that old familiar strain on your mind and emotions.

You can experience stress from moving, the environment, your body, and your thoughts. Stress is mostly caused by uncomfortable changes, but even positive changes like promotion, a new house, or the birth of a child can be a stressor.

But how do we recover from stress?

There are several things that can help, but God wants us to turn to Him first, and then He will direct our path, as Proverbs 3:5-6 describes.

God's ultimate goal is for us to have peace in our lives, but we have to follow Him to find it. The book of Proverbs is full of words of wisdom and peace.

9

Proverbs 3:5-6 sounds very comforting. When you first read it, you might think, "I do that!"

But do you really?

Do you trust God at all times? Or do you sometimes rely "on your own understanding"?

Stop and think about that one. Yes, it's human nature to lean "on your own understanding" when stresses in life arise.

What is understanding, anyway? According to the Bible, two different themes surround the true definition of understanding: God's understanding, which includes knowledge of Himself and ourselves, and Satan's understanding, which includes knowledge of the world.

Satan holds the seat as the prince of this world, so anything of the world is mostly made of Satan's understanding. In the ongoing spiritual battle, Satan wants us to have the world's understanding, and God wants us to have His understanding. This has been a battle ever since Adam and Eve fell into temptation and sin in the Garden of Eden.

Satan's primary purpose is to lure us away from the ways of God just as he tempted Eve with the snake. The media and other influences shape the minds of Christians, to think and act like those who shape the culture we live in.

But where is that stress coming from?

Let's explore areas of life that could be culprits of stress.

Stress of finances

Money can create stress that hangs over your shoulders. But who would blame you for it?

Picture this all-too-realistic scenario: you support several kids by working hard at your job every day, trying to get by.

But then, news arrives that the company may be laying people off. This can start the worry cycle.

I have a close friend who is a single mom who recently lost her job. This caused many trials and stressors. Her young son was in a costly private school, and she didn't want to disrupt his world by pulling him out. That would create even more stress. She thought she would land a job quickly, but it took many months.

Her worry turned into anxiety, which snowballed into stress that eventually snowballed in to anger and bitterness. She was so frustrated that she stopped giving prayer requests and secluded herself.

Fortunately, she was directed to follow God more closely and began searching the Bible for words of guidance. This opened her eyes to actually asking God, "What are you trying to teach me through this long waiting period of disappointment after disappointment?"

Slowly, she gained understanding of how God was working to remove some bitterness she had in her life, and piece by piece, the crusty chips of anger were loosed from her mind.

She softened, and by the time she landed an amazing job, she was faithfully following in God's path, which Proverbs 3:5-6 says God will make straight.

Think about it; have you ever hiked and come upon a winding, crooked path? It was not fun, right?

Once you got to a straight path, there was a sigh of relief. This represents how God works in our lives, but my friend needed to be redirected to hear God's voice in the Bible to get on that straight path.

Stress of learning to follow God

In the Bible, Abraham is an excellent example of dealing with stress while learning to follow God. He lived with his parents and distant relatives, which was the cultural norm in that day, and they all worshipped idols.

When God called Abraham privately to leave his family and follow Him, Abraham might have thought, "What am I doing? I can hear this God, but nobody else can hear Him." But Abraham set out to follow God wholeheartedly, keeping his "eyes fixed on the prize" of life with the eternal "I am." He knew that God would be faithful.

Day by day, Abraham's relationship with God grew stronger as he discovered how much he needed to trust God in every situation. Yes, he went through stressful times, especially when his wife Sarah was almost taken by a king to become his wife, but Abraham kept seeing God's favor through impossible moments.

This concept of releasing your stresses and putting them in God's hand applies to every individual on earth.

Have you recognized God's grace at any points in your life? Have you set your trust in Him, even though sometimes it seems like He doesn't answer?

If you study and analyze events in the Bible, asking God's Spirit to open your eyes to His truth, you can get an idea of how God handles stresses in life, thus becoming more comfortable to lean on His understanding and not your own.

Stress of health struggles

Today, many people in the world, young and old, are beset by diseases. You might have a child with special needs, needing frequent doctor appointments, therapy, and expenses.

One of my close friends was faced with a shock when she had her third child. She had gone through the birth process twice, with healthy children both times, so she wasn't expecting a glitch in the routine. But she was shocked by a child born with Down syndrome.

Her mind was filled with emotions of doubt and future planning: What will the family dynamic look like from now on? Where will I get answers? The stress of the unknown mounted high in her mind.

She kept clinging to God for help and dove into His word.

She managed to jump though hurdle after hurdle to make it through by the grace of God.

Now her child is an adult and is actually getting married soon. Even though her child will never be totally independent in life and will constantly need some form of supervision, this experience caused her to cling tighter to God and lean on His understanding and not her own.

In the Old Testament, good King Asa did not set a good example of depending on God for his health in his old age.

In his earlier years, the prophets had encouraged him to follow God wholeheartedly. "Listen to me, Asa, and all Judah and Benjamin: the Lord is with you when you are with Him. And if you seek Him, He will let you find Him; but if you forsake Him, He will forsake you." (2 Chronicles 15:2) In response, Asa had removed abominable idols from new territories that he gained, which pleased God.

But years later, when Asa had foot disease, he did not seek the Lord. (2 Chronicles 16:12) Instead, he asked physicians first. Now, that's not to say that you shouldn't go to the doctor when you get sick, but God wants you to turn to Him first. If you pray while laying your requests before God, you'll learn how to ask God for help.

When you're too stressed to voice your requests, it may help to write them. Ask God to heal you and guide you to the best treatments for the ailment.

God is the great physician who can heal any diseases because He is the creator of the universe. If you ask God about it first, you'll gain a greater insight into the choice you must make.

God will pave the way for you, but only if you ask.

Stress of relationships

What happens when your adopted teenager rebels and runs off to look for love in all the wrong places?

I have a friend who adopted a beautiful baby girl, who as a teenager felt the pangs of desiring to know why her birth parent gave her up. Many times, this can cause an anxiety that drives the child to look for fulfillment of that love gap caused by a birth parent.

She went after boys in person and when things didn't go her way she went to the internet, which can be very dangerous.

This girl had many encounters with guys of various ages. But the breaking point happened when a stranger came to her house in the middle of the night. To her shock, my friend found this stranger hidden in her daughter's closet.

My friend panicked. Her relationship with her entire family was affected, not to mention her teenage daughter.

My friend, as the worried mom, insisted on leaning on her understanding which is the pattern of the world, and it caused her to spin her wheels for a while. She couldn't see what God was doing in the background, so she tried to hold the reins herself. She allowed her disappointments to consume her thinking.

In the end, she found out that her efforts and worrying did not help at all. Fortunately, they finally got some help from different programs, and their daughter is doing well now.

She discovered that leaning on God's understanding causes less stress for the entire family.

In the New Testament, Jesus had disappointment after disappointment in His relationships. Many people followed Him, because Jesus could perform miracles like producing bread for thousands, but then they turned away from Him.

Even Jesus' disciples, His closest followers, turned away from Him due to fear of being labeled and killed. Even Jesus' siblings didn't believe in Him at first.

Jesus felt the rejection and stress in relationships. But what did He do about it? Did He throw in the towel and say "I'm done with God the Father and I refuse to do what I was sent to earth to accomplish"?

No, Jesus took time to reflect with God the Father so He could refill with calmness instead of stress. In order to overcome stressful situations, He isolated himself from the causes of those stressors and got alone with God.

Stress of death

A friend of mine married his high school sweetheart and lived happily with a couple of children. But then a sudden accident took the wife's life. This loss crushed the children and left the family all hanging in confusion.

Why would God let that happen?

It's important to remember that we live in a broken world. Satan came to earth to steal, kill, and destroy, beginning when he brought death to Adam and Eve, who were intended to live in a world of paradise forever. The act that caused them to fall into sin broke the paradise and brought death.

So what about the spouse left alone? What happens to them? If they can learn to follow God wholeheartedly, then they can grow stronger from their loss. God will always bring good out of tragedy and loss, even if you may not realize it at the time.

Physical stressors

If you have an injury from an accident or trauma from childhood abuse, the stress of having to deal with this pain day after day can be grueling.

A well-known example of someone experiencing ongoing physical stress is Nick Vujicic. Nick was born without any arms or legs.

Throughout his childhood, Nick struggled with depression and loneliness, constantly wondering why he was different than all the other kids. He questioned the purpose of his life.

But at age 19, he began speaking all over the globe, inspiring people to press on following God wholeheartedly despite the daily struggles you face. Giving the credit to his faith in God, family, friends and the many people he has encountered along his life journey, Nick travels the world telling his story.

He has impacted millions of lives all over the world.

Nick is an example of someone who did not let his physical stressors stop his life from being used by God.

In the Bible, Paul is one of the best examples of a person who dealt with physical stress. The Bible says he had a thorn in his flesh and prayed continually that God would remove this thorn. It must have been excruciating and maybe even hindered Paul's writing much of the New Testament or physically deterred him in his travels to spread the good news of salvation.

Whatever the case, God would not remove Paul's thorn from his flesh. So why do you think God wouldn't answer Paul's prayers and take away his thorn? After all, Paul served Him wholeheartedly and sacrificially.

From what we can observe in Scripture, we can pick up that God's purpose was to remind Paul that he was weak, and God was strong.

God's goal for all of us is that we serve Him as Jesus served Him. He wants us to follow the example of Christ in all that we do. By seeing that His ways are so much higher and better than our ways, we can begin to deal with physical stressors as Paul did.

Jesus said in Matthew 11:28-30, "Come to Me, all you who are weary and heavy-laden, and I will give you rest. Take My yoke upon you and learn from Me, for I am gentle and humble in heart, and you will find rest for your souls. For My yoke is easy and My burden is light." That is what God has been asking us all to do, lean on His understanding with His yoke, not our own.

Sometimes God has to work to get our attention, to get through our thick skulls, our need to follow Him. That may be why the physical burden lasted Paul's entire career for God.

If you have a physical stressor, ask God to teach you through your ordeal. Maybe along this path, you'll gain wisdom and knowledge about God that you never knew before.

Taking a minute to explore Proverbs 3 is vital to understanding how to deal with stress. It says "Trust in the Lord with all your heart" and then tells us how to trust in the Lord: by not leaning on our own understanding.

So, when trials and tribulations come our way, what do we do? Should we go into a tailspin of thoughts about our dilemma and care more about things of this world than about eternal things?

According to Proverbs 3:5-6, God wants to change this mind-wandering. These verses command us to trust in God and teach us how to trust in God, by not leaning on our own understanding.

 ## Applications

Read Matthew 6:25-34.

1. According to Matthew 6:25, what are two things we're told not to worry about?

2. How do these two things affect your daily stress?

3. According to Matthew 6:26, how can you know that you can trust God?

4. According to Matthew 6:27, do worrying and stressing extend your life?

5. According to Matthew 6:33, what must we do to acquire the things we worry about?

6. According to Matthew 6, should we be worrying about our future tomorrow?

7. In reflection, how much of your day is spent worrying about your future?

 ## Actions

Pray

Ask God to teach you to trust Him and lean on His understanding. Next time something important comes up in your mind, ask God to help you consciously learn through that dilemma.

It takes practice to give every thought to God, which may seem difficult at first but will eventually fill you with peace. Those stressful scenarios in your head can be replaced with, for example, praising God for all of His amazing attributes like Savior, Shepherd, Healer, All-knowing, All-powerful, Worthy, Honor, Praise, Peace, Joy, Rock, and many more.

Recognizing God's attributes is one way to begin your journey in leaning on God's understanding. Picture yourself in God's hand instead of that comfy hammock on the cover of this book.

He's there for you every step of the way, and His goal is to teach you 2 Corinthians 10:5 that says "We are destroying speculations and every lofty thing raised up against the knowledge of God, and we are taking every thought captive to the obedience of Christ." Holding your thoughts captive is what God wants for your life, and if you trust in Him daily, you will see that He upholds His promises.

Be still

Jesus regularly escaped to quiet places to remember that His Father said, "Be still, and know that I am God." (Psalm 46:10 NKJV) He needed to escape from the stresses of the world to get alone with God. We need to pray as we go throughout our day, but we also need to get alone with God. There's nothing like escaping from the crowd to your quiet place where you can shut a door and basically shut the world out.

Remember, God is the only One who can truly fill you with joy. Psalm 16:11 says, "You will make known to me the path of life; In Your presence is the fullness of joy; In Your right hand there are pleasures forever." We can always count on our Creator.

Make a "Top Five" list

Write down the top five stressors in your life and take the list to a special prayer place in your house. Lay out the paper and talk to God about it. Ask Him to keep these stresses from causing you to worry. Pray something like this: "Dear God, here is my stress on paper. Please take it from me and do Your will. Teach me to live the life You want me to live. Take away my worries. Amen!"

Now that we've identified the problem of stress, let's talk about why stress exists in the next chapter called "Desires."

CHAPTER 2

Desires

James 1:12-17
"Blessed is a man who perseveres under trial;
for once he has been approved,
he will receive the crown of life which the Lord has promised
to those who love Him.
Let no one say when he is tempted,
'I am being tempted by God';
for God cannot be tempted by evil,
and He Himself does not tempt anyone.
But each one is tempted when he is carried away and enticed
by his own lust.
Then when lust has conceived, it gives birth to sin;
and when sin is accomplished, it brings forth death.
Do not be deceived, my beloved brethren.
Every good thing given and every perfect gift
is from above,
coming down from the Father of lights,
with whom there is no variation or shifting shadow."

In Matthew 6, Jesus suggested that stress can make it difficult to follow God wholeheartedly. And now James 1:12-17 is telling us to persevere under trial.

If everything in your life always went perfectly, then you could become self-sufficient. When you're self-reliant, then you won't follow God wholeheartedly.

Does that seem to happen to you? When everything in life goes smoothly, needing God's help can fall to the last thought on your mind.

The most outstanding examples of followers of God in the Bible were people who had to learn to persevere under stress and trials.

James 1:13-14 says that God does not tempt us, but that we are enticed by lust. When you study the word *lust*, you'll see that its synonyms connect to the word *desire*: "to crave, covet, want, wish for, long for, yearn for, hunger for, thirst for, ache for, burn for, and pant for." When "lust" refers to "selfish desires," stress can often result.

Luke chapter 10 tells the story of Martha, who was preparing dinner for Jesus. She wanted it to be a beautiful meal and may have gotten frazzled, the way we might get frazzled at a holiday celebration or a birthday party. When her sister Mary sat at Jesus' feet, Martha wanted her to help so that everything would go smoothly at the meal.

Have you ever gotten so worked up over the details of events going smoothly that you snapped at your kids or lashed out at your spouse or family? Was the beautiful dinner worth the anger?

What if you had thought to lean on God's understanding and follow Him instead? Maybe those harsh words could have turned into loving words that build up loved ones.

Three reasons we feel stressed

We have wrong desires

"Every good thing given and every perfect gift is from above, coming down from the Father of lights, with whom there is no variation or shifting shadow." (James 1:17)

Do you think about how every good thing you experience comes from God? Even if you or someone else plays a part in the good thing (working hard, showing love, etc), ultimately it all goes back to God. In the Old Testament, the people of Israel often forgot that every good thing comes from God. God blessed them in many ways, but then they forgot God.

The result of forgetting God was that they would be overrun by their enemies and ultimately would call out to God in their stressful dilemma. He was always faithful to come to their rescue.

Then when things were good again, they would forget that God was the only source of their blessings and abundance. These actions became a cycle, and God's people would again fall prey to the pagan neighbors. They even got to the point of worshiping their false gods and offering God's abundant supply of food and wine to these pagan idols.

The underlying problem was that they refused to remember who supplied all their needs.

In a way, this can happen to us too. Do you find that when you're enjoying your blessings, you sometimes forget God? Because people in the world can appear successful and "cool," you might be tempted to follow their ways and not God's.

Maybe you've noticed some Hollywood actors who sell out to the world and seem to have a great life full of glamour. But eventually they crash and then the tabloids are riddled with their heartbreaks, reminding us that following the world instead of God is not worth it. It reminds us to lean on God's understanding and not the world's understanding.

We don't ask

When God's Old Testament people, the Israelites, wanted more delicacies like the pagans and joined them by turning to their idols, they made the huge mistake of neglecting to ask God to fulfill their needs. If they had asked God, they would have seen Him provide in surprising ways.

Second Samuel 11 tells the story of King David going for a walk on his roof instead of going to war the way he should have. When he was there, he saw a beautiful woman named Bathsheba bathing on her own rooftop some distance away. Overcome with feelings of lust, David didn't talk to God about this temptation; instead, he called his men to bring Bathsheba to him. When he found out she was the beloved wife of one of his soldiers, it didn't seem to matter to him. He was overcome with the desire to get what he wanted when he wanted it. Immediately!

When Bathsheba became pregnant, David tried to cover the sin by ordering her husband's death in battle.

David was tempted and didn't stop to ask God for help. This resulted in many sins of trying to cover up his sin.

This example of David teaches us always to ask God to help us with every temptation. The consequences of sin are not worth it, and they affect everyone around us.

Always ask God first.

We don't seek God's will

Sometimes our minds can get caught up in enjoying the many material pleasures we have, and then wanting more. I've met many people who aren't happy with what they have, because their lives are spent striving for things that they don't have.

Are these material things worth all that striving effort?

When I was in the 5th grade, I got a radio for Christmas. The speakers were set up to let me create the innovative feature of "surround sound." At the time, it was the kind of gift my friends envied, but only a few years later technology had changed so much that this wonderful gift didn't have much relevance.

Has that kind of thing ever happened to you?

Or how about that dream relationship you might have fantasized about? It didn't happen the way you pictured, and all the dreaming only increased the disappointment.

In reality, God's will is best for you. It may take waiting on God, but He knows what is best for you. We were created to lean on God's understanding and not our own.

Kids in a toy store may want every toy in sight, but you know that would never give them lasting happiness. So even if you could afford to buy everything in the store, you might wisely hold back and allow them to choose one toy.

God is the same way; He doesn't let us have everything we want in life because He knows better than we do. God's will is to teach us to be satisfied following Him, loving Him, getting to know Him, and doing His will. His ways are always higher than ours, and we need to remember that He is the source of perfect things in life that are lasting.

If we refuse to listen and seek our own selfish desires, then we might throw temper tantrums like a spoiled kid in a toy store. Those tantrums will keep us from seeing what God has hidden for us in His perfect will. We have to take steps to learn how to desire following God.

Giving it to Him

I once saw a picture of a little child holding a teddy bear talking to Jesus. His hand was extended towards the toy as if He were going to take it away. The little girl said, "But I love it, Jesus," and Jesus replied, "Just trust me."

What the little girl didn't see was that Jesus was holding a bigger and better teddy bear behind His back. If we don't trust God that He has bigger and better gifts for us, "hiding behind His back," then we'll never truly understand the meaning of happiness; we must lean on God and allow the stress to fall away, for all is in God's hands.

In Luke 19, Zaccheus was a selfish tax collector who pursued his own selfish desires. As a chief tax collector, countless times he committed extortion, which allowed him to have a fancy house with all the best provisions.

When Zaccheus heard about Jesus, the Messiah promised in the Old Testament scriptures, he had a sudden desire to pursue Him. Because of all his sins, this tax collector felt extremely unworthy, so he hid in a sycamore tree to gaze at the Lord Jesus from afar.

But to Zaccheus's surprise, Jesus saw him in that tree and understood why he was hiding. Once Zaccheus met Jesus, he wanted to follow so wholeheartedly that he promised to give back all that he had stolen from people plus extra money for their loss.

Before meeting Jesus, Zaccheus was not asking God for help and was not doing God's will.

However, once he understood the fulfilling promises that Jesus gives, Zaccheus finally found the best path instead of listening to his selfish desires.

Applications

Read Psalm 37:3-4, Luke 19:1-10.

1. According to Psalm 37:3-4, how do we get what our hearts desire?

2. When Jesus called up to Zaccheus in the tree in Luke 19:5-6, what attitude did Zaccheus have towards Him?

3. In Luke 19:7, how did the other people react to Jesus' compassion towards Zaccheus?

4. According to Luke 19:8, what did Zaccheus promise to do after he repented of his sin?

5. What did Jesus promise Zaccheus in verse 9?

6. According to Luke 19:10, why did Jesus come to earth?

7. After reading Luke 19, do you think Zaccheus delighted in the Lord as described in Psalms 37:3-4? Do you delight in the Lord?

Actions

Prayer book

Order the *Ashley T Lee Prayer Book* online or use paper or a notebook. Keep it at your prayer spot, where you can write down your prayer requests.

Ask God for everything, whether big or small. Jesus said in Matthew 7:7, "Ask, and it will be given to you; seek, and you will find; knock, and it will be opened to you."

Some people avoid doing this because they think it's too selfish to ask for what you desire, but God wants every part of our minds. You can ask God to show you if you're asking with a selfish motive. But if you never ask God but keep mind drifting about your desires, that's even worse.

I remember as a new Christian starting this routine of writing down prayer requests. At first I asked for everything, and after a while, God changed my desires to become more in line with His desires. So, I found myself asking for less, and for more important things, things of eternal spiritual value.

If I had never asked for these things, then He wouldn't have been able to deal with me as quickly because my heart wouldn't have been open to His directions and will.

When you start writing down all your requests, you'll begin to see how you can learn to lean on God's understanding.

Writing your desires will help you identify your "mind drifting" so God can direct you in His will. That's what the next chapter is about.

CHAPTER 3

Mind Drifting

Proverbs 3:6-7
"In all your ways acknowledge Him,
And He will make your paths straight.
Do not be wise in your own eyes;
Fear the Lord and turn away from evil. "

Where does your mind go?

Do you consistently acknowledge God in your mind, or do you find yourself "mind drifting" instead?

Of course, we need to search out answers for the future, but it's important to keep God's word in the loop. When our mind is consumed about too many "what ifs," that can lead to a life of worry and not trusting God. We can become overcome with fear. This is what Satan wishes for us to do.

Our minds can also drift to what we don't have and can't get, which can lead to deep dissatisfaction and even sin. If we run off into thinking like the world recommends, many times it will be contrary to God's plan. Mind drifting may seem appealing, but ultimately it can lead to trouble.

The enemy wants to fight us. First Peter 5:8 says, "Be of sober spirit, be on the alert. Your adversary, the devil, prowls around like a roaring lion, seeking someone to devour."

I often find my mind wandering, and if I'm not careful I'll catch myself actually falling into a trap of sin that could include lust, envy, strife, or excessive worry.

The key in situations like this is to ask God to capture our thoughts and teach us to think like Him. This is what it means to lean on God's understanding.

The tailspin of mind drifting creates stress, worry, and sinful thinking. After experiencing this awful mind drifting feeling of anxiety, it should be self-evident why continuous mind drifting is hazardous to one's mental health in the Lord.

Do you jump to conclusions?

Jumping to conclusions can affect your relationship with others, with yourself, and with God by creating false findings that can damage your mindset about reality regarding others and even God. Whether it be in a romantic, long-term relationship or a regular interaction with a stranger, jumping to conclusions can lead to deep trouble.

But if you lean on God's understanding and follow His pattern of thought, then the future can be beautiful. But be prepared when you begin to follow God diligently, He may allow trials and tests to grow your faith. Sometimes that might involve rigorous and grueling training like a soldier or ambassador. Though you may not look forward to these hardships, keep in mind that your relationship with God is the only perfect relationship. God is perfect, He never changes, He always loves you unconditionally, and He's always there for you through prayer and petition.

So with all of those beautiful promises in mind, trials and sufferings are worth the risk to encounter and overcome.

The futility of mind drifting

Picture the CEO of a successful company who thinks he has it all: money, dream job, and perfect family. But day by day, he continues to let finances and business dealings cause stress and worry that overcome his time. He then turns to the what-ifs of mind drifting, wishing for something better and more significant, even though he currently has so much.

This lack of satisfaction, which could be a void or "God-shaped hole" in his heart, might lead the CEO into a state of mind drifting for hours, thinking of things that he can do to make more and get more.

If this man wrote down his wish and showed it to God, how would God respond?

God sees all our flaws and sins, but He offers grace to those who put their faith and trust in Him. So why not bring all of your worries and stresses to God? He will help you no matter what the situation, as long as you make the decisions through Him and not just yourself.

All the worry and stress can be debilitating and many times causes ulcers or headaches. So, to avoid the stress of mind drifting and feeling like you are the only one in the world who is making these decisions, turn to God instead.

A crucial question to ask is, "What do I seek in life?" Is it winning the lottery, or becoming famous? How much time do you waste mind drifting about these desires?

According to King Solomon, the wisest man who ever lived before Jesus, this is all vanity. Solomon sought to be the best at everything on his own, but he learned towards the end of his life, while writing Ecclesiastes, that if he didn't follow God while seeking the desires from Him, then he was grasping at the wind and blowing to and fro in chaos.

Most succeeding kings didn't listen to Solomon's advice, so they didn't acknowledge that everything good comes from God. Many of them modeled a life of worshiping idols like Solomon did and sacrificed delicacies to idols hoping to gain more delicacies. But when put into perspective, this makes little to no sense at all. God provided corn, oil, and wine, and yet the kings took these gifts and laid them on an altar to idols made of wood, stone, and gold, hoping they could get more. Insane, right?

Well, have you ever caught yourself compromising your morals or being dishonest to gain? The prophet Elijah showed how vain these efforts were when he called down fire from heaven and God licked up a water-drenched altar with a fire. Eight hundred fifty pagan prophets danced around the altar all day long crying out to their false gods and cutting themselves, hoping to prove their gods were alive. But because this was evil, God gave a miraculous and astonishing display of His power.

Time and time again, God has shown that He is the only true living God. He continually proved that He is the single source of good things.

Common mind-drifting examples

Mind drifting in relationships

Many times, people fantasize about a potential relationship without discussing it with God. But God sees our lives as if He were watching a parade from a blimp: while our view is very limited as to what lies ahead, He can see everything the future holds.

When it comes to dating and relationships, it's easy to jump into thinking, "This could be the one!" But in reality, there are several questions to ponder in situations like this, like "Have I gotten to know the person on a spiritual level? Have I asked God what He thinks? Have I spent time getting to know the person's friends and family? Is this relationship infatuation? Does the other person feel the same way about me?"

These aspects of a relationship are all critical for it to be able to survive and flourish.

Mind drifting regarding starting a family

Mind drifting can also happen when young couples are trying to decide if they should start a family. They can toil for hours imagining the future and wondering what they should do. But if they turn and ask God, they could avoid stress and worry. By leaning on His understanding and not the world's, answers will come. With the world influencing your decisions about almost everything, it is crucial that for essential matters such as children, you should turn to God for answers.

Mind drifting in prayer time

Another mind-drifting nightmare happens when you go to your prayer place to be quiet and still before God, but your mind becomes jumbled with unimportant matters like errands you have to run or what you need to do later in the day.

But think about this…what if young David had been tending his sheep, and instead of praising God by singing and writing psalms, he was talking with a girlfriend or texting his stockbroker?

It's not that it's terrible to text people or do an exchange with a stockbroker, but if you can't be still long enough to see and hear God, then you'll be focused on guidance from the world rather than God. If David had done these things instead of talking with God, his mind wouldn't have been still long enough to listen and learn. The same applies to us.

Psalm 46:10 (NKJV) says, "Be still and know that I am God." How can you know God if you don't get still enough to concentrate and focus on Him? Ask Him to teach you to be still. Then after prayer time and reading His words in stillness, you'll be able to meditate and think upon the things of God all day. You'll find it easier to follow God and lean on Him if you can be still and know God.

Examples we can learn from

The bad example of Judas

In the Bible, Judas, one of Jesus' disciples, was an example of someone who didn't keep his mind from drifting. He was swayed by Satan to mind drift into a fairyland of wealth, to the point where he betrayed Jesus for thirty pieces of silver.

Satan may have made some impressive promises to him, but sadly, once Judas fell into sin, his life ended. Satan had used him to accomplish Jesus' death, and then he was done with Judas. If Judas hadn't allowed his mind to be pulled away, he wouldn't have gone down in history as the most notorious traitor ever.

The bad example of King Saul

After David killed the giant Goliath and was lauded by the people, King Saul became so jealous of David that he kept on pursuing him to have him killed.

Saul's desire to be worshiped by the people meant he disobeyed God's commands given through Samuel the prophet. Saul worked so hard to kill David that he even tried to kill his own son, who helped David. His fear overcame him to the point that late in his life when he couldn't hear from God, instead of repenting he got a prophecy from a witch. Saul's mind drifting was so terrible, eventually it destroyed him.

The good example of Jesus

While Jesus was on earth, He often left the crowds to be alone with His Father. He didn't mind drift like we do because He was always leaning on God's understanding. Then, when Jesus was about to go to the cross, He said to His Father in Matthew 26:39b, "not as I will, but as You will." As Jesus was sweating blood and His mind as a human was drifting, He brought His thoughts back to leaning on God's will and understanding.

We need to follow His example for us, but if we don't take time to be still and listen to His words, then we will never find out what our standard of Christ looks like.

"Fear the Lord and turn away from evil"

Running off into mind drifting can tailspin into a trap of fear, worrying about what people think and then worrying and fearing about our future.

Proverbs 3:7b warns us to "fear the Lord and turn away from evil." Mind drifting can lead to sinful thinking instead of healthy thinking. To prevent sinful thoughts that result from mind drifting, make sure to dwell in prayer, ask God for protection, and praise Him for all the blessings He has given you.

Philippians 4:8 says, "Finally, brethren, whatever is true, whatever is honorable, whatever is right, whatever is pure, whatever is lovely, whatever is of good repute; if there is any excellence or if anything is worthy of praise, dwell on these things."

I went through a stage in my walk with God where I fell into fear and found myself dwelling on fearful thoughts. My mind was on a tailspin of pessimism and fear. One day I was thinking about how to change my thought process, and I remembered as a newer Christian learning Philippians 4. Other Christians said to use it when you feel depressed or sad.

I got out the verse, wrote it on index cards, listened to it, and ultimately memorized it. Whenever my mind went into its tailspin I kept saying it over and over, and it worked!

Take time to "dwell on these things" in Philippians 4:8.

Weapons against mind drifting

When we tailspin into mind drifting, we're actually trying to create something out of our own efforts, when all along God is in control.

2 Corinthians 10:3-6 tells us "For though we walk in the flesh, we do not war according to the flesh, for the weapons of our warfare are not of the flesh, but divinely powerful for the destruction of fortresses. We are destroying speculations and every lofty thing raised against the knowledge of God, and we are taking every thought captive to the obedience of Christ, and we are ready to punish all disobedience, whenever your obedience is complete."

Second Corinthians 10:5 tells us to take "every thought captive to the obedience of Christ."

This can be very hard to do. The fast pace of life makes it difficult not to run off on these types of thoughts about the unknown future.

In today's society, we have such a variety of choices, which makes us believe we can narrow down to get the exact thing we desire. From food courts to online stores, we think we can figure out what we want in our future; yet that is not the truth, which can make life frustrating.

In this scripture, Paul warned the followers of God to watch out for speculations and deceptive fantasy thoughts that can be destructive to God's truths. If we tailspin into these thoughts, they will keep us from following God and pull us into a trap of leaning on our understanding and not God's understanding. The depression and disappointment that results from this tailspin trap can be devastating.

But this verse tells us that we have weapons that are not only mighty enough "for the destruction of fortresses," but are strong enough to hold "every thought captive to the obedience of Christ."

The word of God can help us hold our thoughts captive to Christ.

 Applications

Read John 21:1-11.

1. According to John 21:5, can you describe how the disciples were drifting out at sea with no success?

2. According to John 21:1 and 4, what did it take for the disciples to stop drifting?

3. Jesus' direction caused what to happen in John 21:6?

4. According to John 21:7, what did Peter do upon realizing it was Jesus speaking to them?

5. Do you follow Jesus wholeheartedly like Peter?

6. In John 21:11, how did the disciples have proof that this act of the nets filling with fish was a miracle from Jesus?

7. After seeing what Jesus did for the disciples, what should your mind drift on in the future? Think about attributes of God.

 ## Actions

Memorize Philippians 4:8

This way when you begin to mind drift you can "dwell on these things" listed in Philippians 4 and not think about destructive mind-drifting things of the world.

Memorize and listen to Psalm 51

One of the best ways to prepare your mind to take "every thought captive to the obedience of Christ" and not to mind drift is to listen to God's word. A perfect place to begin is Psalm 51. You can memorize it more easily by listening to it on a loop by using the Bible app at www.fighterverses.com.

King David wrote Psalm 51 after he committed adultery with Bathsheba. The prophet confronted him, and he repented towards God. Many people find it very difficult to confess their sin and guilt. Admitting that you've done something wrong makes you vulnerable. But that's the point with Psalm 51. God wants you to be vulnerable with Him, and He wants to strip down your sin so that He can have a transparent, open relationship with you.

Imagine if you cheated on your spouse. You might have felt sorry about cheating, but you didn't want to tell them. Then, as much as you tried in that relationship, it could never be transparent because you knew that you had cheated and you were holding on to that secret.

Until the secret is out on the table, the relationship can never be open and restored. The same is true with God. Until we open up to Him and reveal our sinfulness, our relationship with Him cannot be complete, and we cannot follow Him wholeheartedly.

In addition to listening to Psalm 51, print it out and write it on index cards. Review it daily and pray it to God. After listening, memorizing, and praying Psalm 51 for a while, you will be amazed at the openness and joy you acquire in the Lord. This psalm is perfect for bringing down strongholds that hold your thoughts captive to the world and not to Christ.

Memorizing Psalm 51 will prepare your heart for His forgiveness, outlined in the next chapter.

CHAPTER 4

Forgiveness

Romans 4:7
"Blessed are those whose lawless deeds
have been forgiven,
And whose sins have been covered."

As we learn to talk to God and follow Him wholeheartedly, we need assurance of His faithfulness. After all, you're much more likely to trust a close companion for advice than a stranger. God wants you to become part of His family so that you grow to follow and trust His advice.

The ultimate way to become part of God's family is to trust in Jesus Christ for your salvation. Then you can look to His perfect word to understand what He expects of you.

When you're born into a truly good family, you know what it means to experience love under all circumstances. Because of this love, you and your family members will want to do what will please and help each other.

It's the same way in God's family. He is delighted in His children and wants to please them with His joyful presence. You'll want to live in the light of His presence and do what pleases Him.

41

God created everyone to have fellowship with Him, but ever since Adam and Eve, sin gets in the way. Abraham, the first follower of God, had a personal relationship with God, so he obeyed Him. Because of his heritage, all of his descendants knew about God, but sin kept getting in the way of a relationship with Him.

If you listened to and studied Psalm 51 in the Actions section in the last chapter, then you saw how King David cried out to God for mercy after he had sinned. God called David "a man after My heart, who will do all My will" (Acts 13:22b) because he followed God wholeheartedly. Yes, he sinned against God, but David never worshipped idols as many of the other kings of Israel had done. For this and other reasons, David received a special covenant with God: the Messiah would descend from his line.

Every year, the people of Israel went to the temple to offer a sacrifice for their sins. But God had promised that one day there would be a final sacrifice for sins. His promise was fulfilled when the Messiah became that final sacrifice, the solution to the problem of sin.

David was so touched that God would find him worthy to be part of the lineage of the Messiah who would come to the earth one day to be that final sacrifice. When he sinned grievously, in Psalm 51 he begged for forgiveness so he could regain fellowship and keep walking with God.

David paid the consequences for his sin for the rest of his life, but God did have mercy on David and forgave him, in spite of his sin.

This chapter looks at Psalm 51 in sections to understand the depth of God's mercy fully.

Looking at forgiveness through Psalm 51

Psalm 51:1-2 (ESV)

"Have mercy me, O God, according to your steadfast love;
according to your abundant mercy blot out my transgressions.
Wash me thoroughly from my iniquity,
and cleanse me from my sin!"

First, let's set the stage.

Instead of going out to fight with his army, King David had chosen to stay home. There he was drawn away, "mind drifting," to ultimately break some of God's most essential laws. When David saw his neighbor's wife bathing on the rooftop, he could have turned away and repented of any lustful thoughts.

But he made a choice. He chose to focus his lust on the beauty of this woman, and he chose to ignore God's moral laws, which state "thou shall not covet" and "thou shalt not commit adultery."

David sent for his servants to bring Bathsheba to himself and violated her. By undertaking this act, David was not upholding his Godly values. Instead, he was choosing to turn away from God's laws.

When David learned that Bathsheba was pregnant, he panicked and conspired to have her husband murdered, adding another broken commandment.

After the prophet Nathan accused David to his face, David was convicted and sorrowful. He asked God to blot out his iniquity and wash him clean.

And God did.

Psalm 51:3-6 (ESV)

"For I know my transgressions, and my sin is ever before me,
Against you, you only, have I sinned
and done what is evil in your sight,
so that you may be justified in your words
and blameless in your judgment.
Behold, I was brought forth in iniquity,
and in sin did my mother conceive me.
Behold, you delight in truth
in the inward being,
and you teach me wisdom in the secret heart."

If you are not a Christian or aren't sure if you have truly repented of your sins, this section of Psalm 51 is important to understand.

David sorrowfully considered his sin and confessed that he had offended a holy and perfect God. He knew that with his sin he could not stand in the presence of God.

In those days, the high priest had to clean himself thoroughly to be able to go into the Most Holy Place once a year, which was the special place in the Temple where God's presence dwelled. As the priest worked, the little bells sewn on his robe would quietly ring.

Tradition tells us that in case the high priest committed any offense while he was in the Most Holy Place, he had to have a rope attached to his ankle so that if God struck him dead, someone could pull him out without having to enter the Most Holy Place.

Anyone who comes into God's presence must have their sins cleaned off. In Psalm 51:4, David acknowledged God's sinlessness when he says, "you may be justified in your words and blameless in your judgment." David knew that a punishment of death would be justified since he had a man killed.

How many of us have killed in our hearts? Jesus said in Matthew 5:21-22 that if we hate someone without cause, it is similar to murder in our hearts. Anyone who is lost needs to be rescued from your sin so that you can live in fellowship with God as a Christian.

In the perfect paradise of the Garden of Eden, where there was no death, sorrow, or pain, Adam and Eve committed the first sins. Then sin became the new normal. The Garden was now an unholy place where unholy acts had taken place.

But God provided a way for Adam and Eve to have a life outside of the Garden, through an animal sacrifice

David also knew that we desperately need a sacrifice—a Savior—in order to ultimately be cleansed, forgiven, and blessed.

But some people are so proud that they refuse to repent of their sin. They say, "Oh, I'll just try to be a good person from now on, and maybe God will overlook my sin." Others say, "I'll try to be good, and hopefully my good deeds will outweigh my bad deeds."

These things are not possible, because God says in Psalm 14:3, "They have all turned aside, together they have become corrupt; There is no one who does good, not even one."

Sin needs to be cleansed, and only God can cleanse sin. God sent Jesus to earth to do the job of dying for the sins of the world. God's plan of redemption is a beautiful picture of mercy and love and forgiveness.

Upon receiving this salvation, learning to lean on God's understanding will come more naturally.

Psalm 51:7-12a (ESV)

"Purge me with hyssop, and I shall be clean;
wash me, and I shall be whiter than snow.
Let me hear joy and gladness;
let the bones you have broken rejoice.
Hide your face from my sins, and blot out all my iniquities.
Create in me a clean heart, O God,
and renew a right spirit within me.
Cast me not away from your presence,
and take not your Holy Spirit from me.
Restore to me the joy of your salvation."

Once David came to grips with the fact that he had grievously sinned against a holy and perfect God, he admitted that he deserved to be cast away from God's presence. He knew he couldn't cleanse his own sin, so he pleaded with God to purge his sin with hyssop and to wash him "whiter than snow." (Psalm 51:7)

The book of Exodus tells us about when God called His people Israel out of Egypt. The night before they were to leave, He commanded them to sacrifice a Passover lamb and use the hyssop plant to paint the blood on the doorposts so the angel of death would pass them by and spare the life of their firstborn. David knew this story, and asked God to cleanse his sins in the same way.

The severity of David's sin caused him to feel as though his bones were all aching and broken. Have you ever felt that way about your sin? Have you ever reached a point where you knew you had grievously sinned against a holy and perfect God?

John the Baptist was the last prophet who paved the way for the Messiah, Jesus. He said what many of the Old Testament prophets had stated, "Repent!" That was always the message, and when people were humble enough to see that they had a problem of sin, they repented and believed in the provision God made for sins. There had to be a blood sacrifice to cover or blot out their sins.

All unsaved human beings have to realize two things: God the Father is too holy to have sin in His presence, and yet He still loves humanity so much that He numbers every hair on our heads. (Matthew 10:30)

Knowing these two things can give us hope: On the one hand, we cannot fix this sin problem, and on the other hand, God loves us so much that He made a way out for us. Through His Son Jesus Christ, He died for all the sins of the world and paid our fine in full.

Jesus came to earth as a man where He could live among sinners, and yet He still kept God's law perfectly for us. Jesus lived a perfect life so that He could be the spotless Lamb for the sacrifice of sins.

David knew that one day the Messiah who descended from him would be born and live on earth. This may have been part of his incentive not to give up on his plea to God for life.

Once we feel this Godly sorrow that brings repentance and believe in Jesus' death and resurrection, then we are assured of our lives forever. God pronounces us "born again" (John 3:3, 3:7), which means we are born into God's family as if we were adopted. Our inheritance is the gift of eternal life. We can live and fellowship with God the way He intended back in the Garden of Eden.

This news of salvation is truly good news. When we trust in Jesus we gain the Holy Spirit, who lives inside us to teach us, warn us, and help us live the life God intended for us.

In the Old Testament, God delivered His Holy Spirit only for a time for people to do His work. David knew he had God's Holy Spirit, but he feared God would take it away due to his sin. That is why He says in Psalm 51, "take not your Holy Spirit from me."

At Pentecost, God's Holy Spirit was delivered to the disciples and others to give them the power to spread the gospel, and today all Christians have this same power that God uses to make us more like Jesus every day and be unafraid to spread His Word.

With humility and leaning on God's understanding, He will make us more like Jesus every day.

Psalm 51:12b-17 (ESV)

"Uphold me with a willing spirit.
Then I will teach transgressors your ways,
and sinners will return to you.
Deliver me from blood guiltiness,
O God, O God of my salvation, and my tongue will sing aloud
of your righteousness. O Lord, open my lips,
and my mouth will declare your praise.
For you will not delight in sacrifice, or I would give it;
you will not be pleased with a burnt offering.
The sacrifices of God are a broken spirit;
a broken and contrite heart, O God, you will not despise."

Our desire to allow God to make us more like Jesus and lean on His understanding is similar to David's experience when he asked God to "uphold me with a willing spirit."

That is what we must do daily to stop worrying and tail spinning in our mind drifting. We must realize that we have to depend on the Holy Spirit to be our helper. If we could figure life out on our own, then why would we need a helper in the first place? (John 14:26)

Once you're saved from sin and death, there is a joy knowing that you are born into God's family, you can enjoy His presence here on earth, and one day you'll go to heaven where there is no sorrow, pain, or suffering, to enjoy His presence more fully.

Christians should teach unsaved people (transgressors) His ways, and cause sinners to return to God, as David says in the scriptures above. After Jesus paid for the sins of the world and rose from the dead, He told His disciples that they needed to spread this good news to their town, surrounding cities, and throughout the world. David's words in Psalm 51 give hints of this beautiful good news to come.

Here's a word picture of the gospel of Jesus Christ displaying this good news: in a courtroom, if you owe a hefty fine that you can't pay, the judge can't legally let you go free. But if someone enters the courtroom with enough funds to cover your fine, then the judge can say "you are free to go."

This is what Jesus did for you. He stepped before God the Judge and paid your fine in full.

If you are not yet a believer in Christ or you know others who are not saved, then here are some things to consider or to encourage your friends to consider.

What will you do now that you know what God did for you? Will you talk to Him and repent of your sin and believe that Jesus indeed died for you and rose from the dead?

Will you consider all of the prophecies from the Old Testament that came true when Jesus died on the cross? There were earthquakes and darkness predicted after He died, and when this happened, many rose from their graves. These facts were even documented by skeptics of that day who did not believe in God.

Jesus came to earth, putting aside His deity, and took all of our punishment for sin on Himself. He died, was buried, and rose from the dead, defeating death and Satan.

The only way sins are forgiven is by a sacrifice. By dying on the cross, Jesus wipes away our sins, if we will repent and believe.

Satan knows that he has been defeated, but he still will regularly come after us to beat us and try to make our lives miserable with stress. That is why it is so important to follow God wholeheartedly after you're saved from sin and death.

 Applications

1. According to Romans 5:8, how much do we know that God loves us, and how did He show us this fact?

2. According to Romans 3:19, what does the law or ten commandments do to our justifying mouth? According to Romans 3:20, what kind of knowledge does the ten commandments or law give us?

3. According to Genesis 3:21, what sacrifice did God make to provide a skin covering for Adam and Eve's sin and nakedness?

4. According to Hebrews 10:11-13 and 19-20, what sacrifice did God make to provide a covering for our sins?

5. According to John 3:16, how do you know that God forgives your sins? Is it something that you can do or did He do it for you?

6. According to Romans 3:10-20, why can we not say "being a good person gets us to Heaven"? According to verse 20, do our good works get us to Heaven?

7. According to Isaiah 53:5-6, Who paid for our sins and brought us blessing and peace for eternity? (See John 19:34, 37.)

 ## Actions

Ask for forgiveness

If you are unsaved, get alone with God in a quiet place or silently where you are now and ask Him to forgive you of your sins. We were all born into sin, and we have all lied, looked with lust, disobeyed parents, or broken God's ten commandments in some other way.

These commandments don't save us—only God can do that. But these commandments are like a mirror to show us all the dirt of sin in our hearts so that we can go to the solution that washes off our sin.

The solution that washes our sin is Jesus Christ, who was God in the flesh who came to sacrifice His life for us. His blood cleans off our sin, and His flesh is our covering from death.

If you never have before, you can pray to God, telling Him that you believe Jesus died on the cross for your sins and you turn from your sins and want Him to wash you clean. At that point of belief, you are born into God's family. The Bible says you're a new creation, you have a new heart, and you'll live forever in fellowship with God. It also says that your sins have been removed "as far as the east is from the west." (Psalm 103:12a)

If you are saved, then pray that you can share this good news with others who need to know.

Romans 6:23 says, "For the wages of sin is death, but the free gift of God is eternal life in Christ Jesus our Lord." Jesus fully paid your fine for past sins, and your gratitude will show in your desire to please Him by living to serve Him.

You'll have help living your life for Him. Upon being saved from sin and death, you'll receive God's Holy Spirit inside you to help you "lean on God's understanding," not your own, and avoid sin.

Memorize

Romans 5:8, "But God demonstrates His own love toward us, in that while we were yet sinners, Christ died for us." Write it on an index card and listen to it on a Bible app for easier memorization.

In Chapter 5, we'll explore how to listen to God's voice so that you can keep following Him wholeheartedly.

CHAPTER **5**

Listen

John 10:14-16
"I am the good shepherd,
and I know My own and My own know Me,
even as the Father knows Me and I know the Father;
and I lay down My life for the sheep.
I have other sheep, which are not of this fold;
I must bring them also, and they will hear My voice;
and they will become one flock with one shepherd."

Throughout the Bible, God uses sheep as an analogy for His people. Psalm 100:3 refers to God's children as "sheep of His pasture," and Isaiah 53:6 says, "All we like sheep have gone astray."

Once we become children of God through the gift of salvation, Christ becomes the One true Shepherd for us.

As Christians grow and mature in our faith by learning to lean on God's understanding, we become familiar with His voice, which is His Word. Romans 10:17 says, "So faith comes from hearing, and hearing by the word of Christ."

The sheep depend on the Shepherd

The ideal shepherd knows his sheep completely, where they need to go, where they can sleep, what they should eat, what predators and diseases they're subject to, and many other things. The sheep learn to trust their shepherd.

But sheep also tend to go astray. They can't always discern what's dangerous.

We as the people of God may also perceive unsafe experiences as safe and promising when, in reality, we're being led astray into the darkness, out of sight from the Shepherd.

Both sheep and God's people are subject to fear, bad choices, and bad habits. We both need a guide. Just as a sheep is wholly dependent on its shepherd, we must be fully dependent on God in everything we do, even when we think we don't need Him.

The Shepherd cares for His sheep

According to John 10:1-10, the Shepherd has two main objectives when it comes to sheep. First, He gathers His flock by leading them faithfully through the door, unlike the thieves and robbers who sneak over the fence with treachery in their hearts.

The Shepherd also guides His flock by communicating salvation through His voice to the sheep so that their lives will be spared. With the hook of His staff, He rescues the sheep from falling in the water while drinking from the brook. He also corrects them when they stray by poking them with his staff so that they don't wander off to possible death.

After Jesus' sermon about sheep and shepherds in John 10, He explained to His listeners that He is the Shepherd. He wanted the crowd to hear His main message: His desire to gather His flock and guide them to salvation. Jesus wants everyone to learn to lean on His understanding so that they can be saved from sin and death. With Jesus as your Shepherd, you can know you'll be provided with great spiritual riches, which are far better than material goods.

But there are false shepherds too.

In Jeremiah 23:1, God says, "Woe to the shepherds who are destroying and scattering the sheep of My pasture!" Then in Jeremiah 23:2 He says to those false shepherds, "You have scattered My flock and have driven them away, and have not attended to them." Crafty false prophets lured God's people like sheep to follow them and leave the flock. God sent the prophet Jeremiah to warn the people to keep following their true Shepherd.

These false shepherds are like the "false prophets, who come to you in sheep's clothing, but inwardly are ravenous wolves" that Jesus warned about in Matthew 7:15. This is important to note as you attempt to follow God more closely.

The flock stays together and follows the Shepherd

In Christian discipleship, experienced believers can help new believers in the congregation (flock) recognize the voice of the Shepherd. We can also bring along non-believers and skeptics, walk beside them, teach them, and always point them to Jesus no matter their response.

However, all humans are imperfect, and this imperfection can lead us astray. Advice from others can be beneficial, but even Christians can sometimes give unwise advice. We need to keep gaining wisdom to recognize the true Shepherd's voice.

As you grow and mature in your faith, you'll want to seek God as your Shepherd and Counselor through His Word. This is what it means to lean on God's understanding and not the world's understanding.

Listening hindrances

Distractions

Throughout history, it has been when people have been "bored" that their thoughts would often turn to spiritual things. Today, though, there is no such thing as being bored. No matter what your mood, trouble, or job, there is something at your fingertips to distract you.

But the distraction of the world within the cell phone can keep us not only isolated from others but also distant from God.

These days, instead of placing God at the forefront of their lives, people are all too often tempted to put these inanimate objects on a pedestal and treat them with praise, almost like idols. Giving all our attention to these distractions will result in a shift in focus from holy activities to worldly choices, from an emphasis on lasting spiritual things to an emphasis on transitory physical things.

Temptations

Just as a sheep pen is set to secure the lives of the sheep, God has put moral boundaries in place for us to protect us. Instead of being punishment or "keeping us from fun," it is a provision of love and concern for our welfare.

For instance, when David violated Bathsheba, committing adultery and murder, God could have taken his life. But when

God sent Nathan the prophet to convict David of his offenses, the purpose was actually to save him.

Temptations now, of pornography, fornication, and adultery, can block God's people from listening to His voice. Pray and ask God to keep you from falling into temptation, and come quickly to Him in repentance if you do.

Stubbornness

Psalm 119:176 says, "I have gone astray like a lost sheep; seek Your servant, For I do not forget Your commandments." Some sheep may want to stubbornly choose their own path, which can lead them astray.

After Jesus rose from the dead, He appeared to some of His followers, who then shared their excitement with the disciple Thomas, who hadn't been there. But Thomas didn't believe them, stubbornly declaring, "Unless I see in His hands the imprint of the nails, and put my finger into the place of the nails, and put my hand into His side, I will not believe." (John 20:25)

Later Jesus appeared again and confronted Thomas, saying (John 20:27), "Reach here with your finger, and see My hands; and reach here your hand and put it into My side; and do not be unbelieving, but believing." When Thomas fell at His feet, Jesus then added, "Because you have seen Me, have you believed? Blessed are they who did not see, and yet believed." (John 20:29)

We must guard ourselves against the kind of stubbornness that prevents our openness to God's truths.

Willful disobedience

When Solomon's son Rehoboam became king, he could have taken the advice of the wise advisors. But instead, he willfully decided to listen to deceitful friends—his "flock," if you will, who led him astray.

King Saul is another example of willful disobedience. Though he had been warned by God's prophet to destroy everything having to do with the Amalekite nation, still he willfully disobeyed, saving some of the best for "sacrifices." As Saul continued to refuse to hear God's voice, God stopped communicating with him altogether, so in desperation he ended up trying to get advice from a witch.

How to listen to God

Get alone with God our Shepherd

Psalm 46:10 (NKJV) says, "Be still, and know that I am God: I will be exalted among the nations, I will be exalted in the earth!"

David is an excellent example of someone who learned to be still in order to listen to God. He spent hours alone with God and would continually "be still" before God as he shepherded the family sheep.

David understood the nature of sheep and knew that God used sheep as an example of the life of man. As David treated his sheep with love and compassion, he grew to understand God's character better. From all of the time David spent with sheep, he wrote many of the most comforting psalms.

Know who He is and what He did for us

God is the "I am." He doesn't change, and He is all-knowing, the Almighty powerful God who came to earth to redeem humankind, His lost sheep.

God loves us as wandering sheep so much that He came to earth as the man Jesus, to live among the sheep, fulfill God's laws, and offer salvation from sin and death.

In the Psalms, David wrote words such as, "Your blessing be upon Your people!" (Psalm 3:8b) and "I have set the Lord continually before me; Because He is at my right hand, I will not be shaken. Therefore, my heart is glad and my glory rejoices; My flesh also will dwell securely. You will make known to me the path of life; In Your presence is fullness of joy; In Your right hand there are pleasures forever." (Psalm 16:8-9,11)

Jesus, the Holy One David was referring to, was the provision that saves us from sin and death. He loves us so much that He left the 99 sheep to seek the one lost sheep (Luke 15:3-7) He is the Shepherd who came to earth to die for the sins of the lost sheep so that we can be saved through Him and have eternal life.

Listen to the Bible (His voice)

Psalm 143:8a says, "Let me hear Your lovingkindness in the morning; for I trust in You;" and Psalm 119:11 (NKJV) adds, "Your word I have hidden in my heart, that I might not sin against You." God speaks to us through His Word—it is a love letter from His heart. If you love Him, you'll want to know Him and recognize His voice. A special thing is to read the Bible in your quiet place or get a Bible app and listen while you're working or driving.

Many Saturday mornings I drive about an hour to go to see my daughter. Often I begin by listening to music, but then remember to turn on my Bible app to listen to it. The blessings I receive when I listen to it are unsurpassed, which makes sense because in Luke 9:35b, God says, "This is My Son, My Chosen One; listen to Him!"

If you want to get close to someone you love, you have to listen to them. Otherwise, there's no fellowship at all. The same is true with God. If we want to experience the blessing of knowing Him in His fulness, then we must listen to Him. His voice is His Word, so listen to it, study it, and hear great preaching of the word of God.

Obey His word – not the world

In the Old Testament, the Israelites wore a headpiece to remind them to obey God's commandments. They also wrote the ten commandments on their doorposts so that when they left their houses and when they returned, they would be re-minded not to steal, bear false witness, covet their neighbor's possessions, and the other commandments.

We also need to be reminded of what God's word says versus what the world says, so that we can make Godly deci-sions and resist the temptation of the world. You can learn to resist the lure of the world by getting to know your Shepherd and obeying His voice in His Word.

Listen to the Shepherd only

There is only one Shepherd, and you have to be still to hear His voice, but sometimes sheep can get caught up with just listening to each other. When your focus is on the flock instead of the Shepherd, this is when it will become easier for false shepherds to deceive.

An example of listening to the Shepherd could be dis-played through a relationship with a spouse. When a husband and wife focus on and depend on each other too much, then they'll begin to be disappointed in each other. Instead, together they can focus on Christ and have Him be the center of the marriage, praying together with God as their counselor. If Christ the Shepherd is the focus, and they love Him together, then in spite of the difficulties life can bring, their relationship will prosper.

Be like the Shepherd

The difference between sheep and humans is that God intends for His people to be transformed to become more like the Shepherd.

The Shepherd is our guide and our counselor, so you should plan on some separate "be still" time with Him. In 2 Corinthians 3:18 we read, "But we all, with unveiled face, beholding as in a mirror the glory of the Lord, are being transformed into the same image from glory to glory, just as from the Lord, the Spirit." In order for us to be transformed the way this verse describes, we need to set aside alone time with our Shepherd.

In my ministry, which includes an app with one-minute teachings for daily devotions, there have been times when God has separated me from the flock. Sometimes I willfully obeyed, and other times He nudged me to follow. Since I'm constantly studying, writing sermons and teachings, life has sometimes gotten very lonely. The entire time, God has been a close Shepherd, ministering to all my needs.

First Kings 17 tells us the story of God calling the prophet Elijah to live by a brook all by himself for over a year. During that year, he learned to trust God for the provision of every bite of food that entered his mouth.

Elijah didn't know it, but God was preparing him for a big job to show the flock, who had been blinded by the enemy, how great their Shepherd was.

There would come a day when, through the work of Elijah, God would show his power and glory by raining fire down from heaven, calling His straying people back to Himself. (You can read about it in 1 Kings chapter 18.)

Many times, during my growing stages in my ministry, I could relate to Elijah being alone at the brook. If God separates you for a time, you can trust that He is preparing you for His work. Stay in His word and be still as He teaches you. Don't fret, because God won't seclude you forever. He'll bring you back to influence His flock, His people.

Keep remembering how He wants us to become more like the Shepherd.

At one point, after a long stretch of loneliness, God opened the door for my one-minute teachings to be played daily on hundreds of Christian radio stations across America. When this happened, it was confirmation that God was separating me to teach me His ways. Sometimes when we go through such a "back side of the desert" experience, we might feel like He is not using us. After what I thought was a dry spell, He finally made it evident what He was actually doing in my life which brought immense joy and peace.

Applications

Read Psalm 23, John 10, and Isaiah 53.

1. According to Psalm 23:1, who is God to us?

2. According to Psalm 23:2-3, what does God do to help you follow Him as your Shepherd?

3.   In Psalm 23:4, why shouldn't we fear evil? What does He use to keep us on track? Tell about a time He used these in your life.

4.   According to Psalm 23:5-6, what are the benefits of following God?

5.   According to John 10:11-15, who lays down His life for the sheep?

6.   According to Isaiah 53:6, what do we do as wandering sheep?

7.   In Isaiah 53:6b-8, who took our punishment for wandering and going astray?

 ## Actions

Get alone with God

Get alone with God to "be still" and know Him better. Carve out time daily to go to a quiet place to pray and write down requests for God. Use the Bible to quote during your prayers, since His Word is how we can listen to God.

Memorize Psalm 23

Psalm 23 will help you know more about God as your Shepherd. You can use www.fighterverses.com to download the memorization app for listening on a loop. Pray Psalm 23 back to God and use it as a tool to fight the teachings of the false shepherds and false sheep who are actually wolves dressed in sheep's clothing.

In Chapter 6, we'll explore how God gifts us with wisdom to follow Him more closely.

Wisdom

Proverbs 3:19-22
"The Lord by wisdom founded the earth;
By understanding He established the heavens;
By His knowledge the depths were broken up,
And the skies drip with dew.
My son, let them not vanish from your sight;
Keep sound wisdom and discretion;
So they will be life to your soul
And adornment to your neck."

Once we begin to learn how to listen to God and lean on His understanding, God will begin to teach us by giving us wisdom through His Holy Spirit.

King Solomon, David's son, was gifted with wisdom from God to rule over the people of Israel. But Solomon didn't apply this wisdom to his relationship with God. Instead, he decided to acquire many foreign wives, he amassed gold and silver, and he even built houses for other gods, contrary to God's commands.

When he was an old man, near death, Solomon wrote, "The conclusion, when all has been heard, is: fear God and keep His commandments, because this applies to every person. For God will bring every act to judgment, everything which is hidden, whether it is good or evil." (Ecclesiastes 12:13-14)

Solomon's heart most likely wouldn't have been turned away, and he probably wouldn't have had so many wives, accumulated so many riches, or built temples to pagan gods if he had only kept his mind and heart focused on God and His word.

Gaining wisdom

Proverbs 3:13 says that the Lord God founded the earth by wisdom. He is the only One who possesses wisdom, and any wisdom we attain is only through Him.

God's wisdom is not something we can attain by our own efforts, but it is given freely by God to those who seek it.

King Solomon's wisdom was granted to him at the beginning of his reign, but he didn't continue to seek it. We can be different from Solomon in that we can continue to seek God.

As we continue to regularly look to God through His word, with the help of His Holy Spirit, we can expect to continue to grow in wisdom.

Gaining wisdom through experience: the Hot Iron Theory

Proverbs 9:10 says, "The fear of the Lord is the beginning of wisdom, And the knowledge of the Holy One is understanding."

God gives us knowledge and understanding, and then we gain wisdom from experience.

In order to picture the Hot Iron Theory, imagine a mother ironing her clothes with her son nearby. When the mother leaves the room, she warns him not to touch the iron because it can burn him. But knowing this, the boy might still be overcome with curiosity and might touch the hot iron. In that instant, the boy gains a deeper awareness of what "hot" means, as the iron sears his flesh.

Now, through experience, he knows his mother told him the truth: that the iron will harm him and must be handled with care. He experiences his mother's love as she puts salve on the burn and bandages it. Then the next time his mother uses the iron, he won't try to touch it. He understands that she gave this instruction for his good. He has grown in wisdom.

It may seem mundane to read the Bible and pray every day in order to know God, but as we pray, God will illuminate His word to us to show us His heart. We'll learn how gently He deals with sinners like us, we'll be eager to get to know Him better, and we'll see that He wants to become our companion in life. All of this is part of learning wisdom.

But wisdom can be "seared" into our hearts through experience. When we go through a hard experience and begin to understand the faithfulness and kindness and love of God in a deeper way, even perhaps when we've disobeyed Him, this is growing in wisdom. We'll know what it means to lean on God's understanding and not the world's understanding.

First Corinthians 1:18-25 (NKJV) says, "For the message of the cross is foolishness to those who are perishing, but to us who are being saved it is the power of God. For it is written: "I will destroy the wisdom of the wise, And bring to nothing the understanding of the prudent." Where is the wise? Where is the scribe? Where is the disputer of this age? Has not God made foolish the wisdom of this world? For since, in the wisdom of God, the world through wisdom did not know God, it pleased God through the foolishness of the message preached to save those who believe. For Jews request a sign, and Greeks seek after wisdom; but we preach Christ crucified, to the Jews a stumbling block and to the Greeks foolishness, but to those who are called, both Jews and Greeks, Christ the power of God and the wisdom of God. Because the foolishness of God is wiser than men, and the weakness of God is stronger than men."

According to this scripture, God has shown that the world's ideas about how to reach Him are foolishness. He has shown us that coming to Him through Jesus Christ to learn wisdom is the only good way.

A few verses later, 1 Corinthians 1:30 tell us that Jesus became for us the "wisdom from God." He is the best way to lean on God's understanding.

Hindrances to gaining wisdom

Too busy to read the Bible

It may seem like with your busy life you don't have any time to read the Bible. But you can ask God to show you where those "little minutes" are that you can reserve for quiet time with Him. It can even be in the car on your way to work or on the way home from dropping the kids off at school. This is the most important way to gain knowledge, understanding, and wisdom from God.

Too busy to take time to pray daily

If you start the day with a psalm, then you can take the words of praise or the attribute of God and pray them in your quiet times. Having a dedicated quiet time is important, but with God you can pray anywhere anytime.

Examples in the Scriptures

The bad example of Ahaz

Ahaz was known for being an evil and immoral King who worshiped idols and burned his children as sacrifices to these false gods. When enemies came against him, Isaiah brought God's words of promise and comfort: "It shall not stand nor shall it come to pass. If you will not believe, surely you shall not last."(Isaiah 7:7, 9b)

With a promise and warning such as these, it would seem that Ahaz would jump at the opportunity to obey God's wisdom and turn from his wicked ways. But instead, he chose not to follow God and was defeated.

The kings had all been instructed to write out the law or God's word with the priest and read it daily. (Deuteronomy 17:18-19) It seems that King Ahaz didn't follow through with reading the word daily, or else he would have gained some knowledge of God, thus gaining understanding and ultimately wisdom. Ahaz showed no sign of welcoming wise words or advice from God's prophet.

The good example of Hezekiah

King Hezekiah got rid of all the idols that his father, Ahaz, had set up and removed worship in high places of pagan gods. He brought back the worship of God and peace to Jerusalem. When the prophet Isaiah was sent to give Hezekiah wise warnings about the enemy attacking, he did the opposite of his father and went into the temple to pray.

In 2 Kings 19:20, Isaiah told Hezekiah, "Thus says the Lord God of Israel, 'Because you have prayed to Me about Sennacherib king of Assyria, I have heard you.'" God miraculously rescued Hezekiah and his people.

Hezekiah's reaction to God's prophet gives an example of wisdom for our benefit.

The bad example of the Pharisees

In the New Testament, the Sanhedrin and Pharisees did not show any signs of wisdom in the way they treated Jesus. John 8:14-19 says, "Jesus answered and said to them, 'Even if I bear witness of Myself, My witness is true, for I know where I came from and where I am going; but you do not know where I come from and where I am going. You judge according to the flesh; I judge no one. And yet if I do judge, My judgment is true; for I am not alone, but I am with the Father who sent Me. It is also written in your law that the testimony of two men is true. I am One who bears witness of Myself, and the Father who sent Me bears witness of Me.' Then they said to Him, 'Where is Your Father?' Jesus answered, 'You know neither Me nor My Father. If you had known Me, you would have known My Father also.'"

Jesus represented wise counsel, but the Sanhedrin and Pharisees couldn't or wouldn't recognize it. If they had truly been seeking God in prayer and hadn't been leaning on their own understanding, they would have seen that Jesus was the fulfillment of all the Bible prophecy.

But because of their stubbornness and pride, they didn't gain the knowledge and understanding they needed to gain wisdom from God to see that Jesus was God in the flesh.

The good example of the early church

As the church grew in number, wisdom was needed. In Acts 6, when deacons were added to the church to take care of the needs of the widows who had no food, the men they chose for the job were all full of the Holy Spirit and wisdom. Wisdom was and still is essential for any role in the church, so it is crucial as Christians that we pursue asking God for wisdom.

Proverbs 2:1-12a gives an excellent overview of wisdom, explaining why the church chose men full of wisdom for service. "My son, if you will receive my words, And treasure my commands within you, Make your ear attentive to wisdom, Incline your heart to understanding; For if you cry out for discernment, Lift up your voice for understanding, If you seek her as silver And search for her as for hidden treasures; Then you will discern the fear of the Lord and discover the knowledge of God. For the Lord gives wisdom; From His mouth come knowledge and understanding; He stores up wisdom for the upright; He is a shield to those who walk in integrity, Guarding the paths of justice, And He preserves the way of His godly ones. Then you will discern righteousness and justice and equity, and every good course. For wisdom will enter your heart and knowledge will be pleasant to your soul; Discretion will guard you, Understanding will watch over you, To deliver you from the way of evil."

God tells us to receive His words and treasure His commands so that we can make our ears attentive to wisdom. Words and commands refer to the Bible, and we gain knowledge from reading the Bible. The Bible is God's voice to us, and Proverbs 2 tells us that from His mouth come knowledge and understanding.

Next, we are to cry out for discernment and knowledge and thus will understand the fear of the Lord, just like the boy with the hot iron.

Once we gain knowledge and understanding from God's Word and prayer, He promises us wisdom.

Our own efforts do not attain wisdom, but it all comes from God. The benefits of leaning on God's understanding and gaining His wisdom is that He guards us and preserves us, delivering us from evil, perverseness, and wickedness. Once we understand this and begin seeking God's wisdom, life becomes an adventure of listening to God and following Him instead of being stressful and burdensome.

Leaning on God's understanding is full of non-stress, peace, and anticipation of God's will for you.

 Applications

1. According to Proverbs 4:7, what must we seek? How do we gain the knowledge for this understanding to happen according to verse 5?

2. According to Proverbs 1:7, how do we gain the fear of the Lord that gives us the knowledge, understanding, and ultimately wisdom from God? Psalm 119:38 and 119:74 give a clue.

3. Who had the greatest God-given wisdom of his day, according to 1 Kings 4:29-30?

4. According to Matthew 12:38 and 42, who has greater wisdom than Solomon?

5. Why does God want us to lean on His understanding instead of the world's understanding, according to 1 Corinthians 1:20?

6. According to 1 Corinthians 2:5, on whom should our faith rest?

7. According to James 1:5, who do we ask if we lack wisdom?

 ## Actions

Pray for yourself

When Jesus was with the disciples, He prayed for Himself first, so how much more should we follow His example? For us to stay focused on doing the things we know God wants us to do like gain knowledge of God's word, seek the Lord and get to know Him, and keep His moral will, we need to pray for ourselves. This world presents so many obstacles that get in the way of our purity and growth in Christ, so the following verses are ones you can take to your prayer place. When we pray for ourselves, God will prepare our hearts to receive the wisdom He intends to give us to do His will.

Here are some scriptures to pray to the Lord.

- Colossians 1:10, "So that you will walk in a manner worthy of the Lord to please Him in all respects, bearing fruit in every good work and increasing in the knowledge of God."
- Colossians 1:11, pray that you will be "strengthened with all power, according to His glorious might, for the attaining of all steadfastness and patience; joyously."
- Ephesians 1:19, "He made known to us the mystery of His will, according to His kind intention which He purposed in Him."
- Ephesians 3:17-19, "So that Christ may dwell in your hearts through faith; and that you, being rooted and grounded in love, may be able to comprehend with all the saints what is the breadth and length and height and depth, and to know the love of Christ which surpasses knowledge, that you may be filled up to all the fullness of God."
- 2 Thessalonians 3:3, "The Lord is faithful, and He will strengthen and protect you from the evil one."
- Matthew 14:35-36, in reference to Jesus, "And when the men of that place recognized Him, they sent word into all that surrounding district and brought to Him all who were sick; and they implored Him that they might just touch the fringe of His cloak; and as many as touched it were cured."
- Romans 6:18, "And having been freed from sin, you became slaves of righteousness."
- First Peter 1:5, Give thanks that you are "protected by the power of God through faith for a salvation ready to be revealed in the last time."

- Job 1:10, 3:23, "Have you not made a hedge about him and his house and all that he has, on every side? You have blessed the work of hands, and his possessions have increased in the land."
- Psalm 32:7, "You are my hiding place; You preserve me from trouble; You surround me with songs of deliverance."

When you use these scriptures in prayer, you can say things like with Job 1, "Lord, please put a hedge around me and my family for protection against my enemy, Satan."

CHAPTER 7

Lay It Down

1 John 3:16
"We know love by this, that
He laid down His life for us; and we ought to
lay down our lives for the brethren."

Once God grants wisdom to us, then we can more naturally live our daily lives humbly surrendering to that God-given wisdom without getting stressed out and frazzled. Laying down our lives before Him and counting on His wisdom to show us the right way to go will help us in living the stress-free life that God wants for us.

Jesus said He laid down His life for us, to save us from sin and death, and now it's our turn to lay down our lives in surrender to His service.

Examples of those who laid down their lives

The example of Mary

Before His crucifixion, Mary came to Jesus to anoint His feet with the most expensive oil she could find.

Why would she have spent her money in such a "reckless" way? This was how much she loved Him, to pour out her sacrifice to honor Him. Because she had little to no money to support herself, Jesus recognized that she had made a massive sacrifice.

Jesus' disciples witnessed this act and thought she was crazy; Judas, the treasurer (who later betrayed Jesus), complained heavily about wasting money.

But Jesus commended and praised Mary's efforts to please and glorify Him. This expensive oil represented her laying down her life before Him.

The example of Paul

Saul encountered Jesus on the road to Damascus. There he laid aside his old life and devoted his new life to spreading the gospel of Christ. Now named Paul, he experienced life-threatening danger for Jesus as he was shipwrecked, beaten, stoned, and kept having to escape from those who wanted to kill him. But he was willing to lay down his life in these ways in order to spread the good news of Jesus' death and resurrection for our salvation. Paul shows us that even the worst sinners can be saved and born again. He also shows what it means to lay down our lives for the sake of others.

The example of Daniel

The Prophet Daniel laid down his life to God by praying three times a day in the pagan land of Babylon, knowing that he was risking his life, with the possibility of being killed for his faith. Eventually he was thrown into a lion's den for praying to the true God, but God saved him as an example for the king and others.

Daniel risked his entire life for God's will and the safety of His people. Daniel's faithfulness to the Lord stands as an example for us today.

The example of King Hezekiah

Just like the hot iron story speaks of gaining experiential knowledge resulting in understanding and wisdom, laying down prayer requests is also important. When we lay out our requests before God, we gain confidence knowing that He is handling our every care, stress, and burden. We can walk away, trusting that our problems are in God's hands, not our own.

Hezekiah was a good king after many bad kings of Judah. Unlike many of his forefathers, he acknowledged and worshiped God, restoring the temple according to its original design.

One day the brutal and terrifying nation of Assyria threatened to attack. When the Assyrian king demanded tribute, King Hezekiah obeyed, even stripping the temple of its gold as some of his ancestors had done, to appease the threatening enemy.

But the Assyrian king decided to take over Jerusalem anyway, and sent a letter telling Hezekiah to surrender. Instead of surrendering, though, Hezekiah took the threatening letter and laid it out in the temple. Isaiah 37:16-20 tells his words: "O Lord of hosts, the God of Israel, who is enthroned above the cherubim, You are the God, You alone, of all the kingdoms of the earth. You have made heaven and earth. Incline Your ear, O Lord, and hear; open Your eyes, O Lord, and see; and listen to all the words of Sennacherib, who sent them to reproach the living God. Truly, O Lord, the kings of Assyria have devastated all the countries and their lands, and have cast their gods into the fire, for they were not gods but the work of men's hands, wood, and stone. So they have destroyed them. Now, O Lord our God, deliver us from his hand that all the kingdoms of the earth may know that You alone, Lord, are God."

Hezekiah was saying, "God I cannot do this. Please take this problem from me and do Your will." God miraculously defeated that enemy.

Hezekiah learned to lay down his life before God and lean on God's understanding. That is God's goal for us also.

How to lay down your life before God

Jesus left His throne in heaven to lay down His life for us so we could have eternal life, as the highlighted verse 1 John 3:16 above describes. He was the promised Messiah who would take away the sins of the world.

Jesus' loving act of crucifixion was as if someone pulled you out of the way of a speeding bus and saved your life, giving His life instead.

But Jesus rose again from the dead, and now, when we have repented and believed in Jesus' work on the cross, we can be filled with the desire to serve Him every day. One way to do that is to lay down our lives for our brothers and sisters, the ones who have believed in Jesus Christ now and the ones who will believe in Him in the future.

Here is how laying down our lives for Jesus can begin.

Get to your prayer place

Make sure you pick a quiet spot to go to every day for prayer. It could be a closet, a special chair, your car, a park, or even the break room at work. Carve out time to go there daily to write down requests and talk to God.

Lay it down

Just like Hezekiah took the threatening letter from the Assyrians to lay it down in the temple before God, Mary poured out her life savings to anoint Jesus' feet for future burial, Paul laid aside his old life to devote it to God by spreading the gospel around the world, and Daniel risked his life to pray three times a day in a pagan land, we can write our requests and stresses to lay before God in prayer.

Here is what laying down our lives as in these examples would look like today:

- Giving up material possessions for God's Kingdom.
- Being willing to suffer to take the gospel to places where it hasn't been heard, which today could be right in your neighborhoods or at local colleges.
- Being willing to endanger our lives for the sake of honoring the Lord.

A great place to start, though, is daily prayer and using the Bible in prayer.

In John 17, Jesus prayed for Himself, then for the disciples, and then for all believers. We can follow His example in our prayers.

Pray for yourself

Praying for Himself Jesus said, "Father, the hour has come; glorify Your Son, that the Son may glorify You." (John 17:1) This prayer is setting an example for us to pray for ourselves first before praying for others.

On airplanes, the announcer says in emergencies to put on the oxygen mask first before putting it on children. It would do no good if the mom passed out and then neither she nor her children could survive. In the case of prayer, we want to be all

God wants us to be before we go out to help others, so we need to ask Him for that, just as Jesus did.

Pray for others

Praying for His closest disciples, Jesus said, "I ask on their behalf; I do not ask on behalf of the world, but for those whom You have given Me; for they are Yours." (John 17:9) Jesus asked God to keep them in His name and not in the world's influence.

This type of prayer can be used for relatives, friends, and others we know. Give all of your emotions for others to God in prayer. Write down requests for everyone around you and lay them down before a holy and perfect God who has all the answers and can act upon our prayers.

What keeps people from prayer

No answers

When you don't find answers after praying ceaselessly about problems, it might be tempting to give up on prayer. A friend once told me, "I prayed about it for the last twelve years and pretty much gave up, because God didn't answer." Little did they know that right around the corner was the most incredible answer they could imagine. God's timing is perfect! Proverbs 16:9 says, "The mind of man plans his way, But the Lord directs his steps." We must remember that God's ways are higher than our ways. (Isaiah 55:9)

Hectic schedules

In today's hectic world, there is often hardly any time left at the end of the day to sit down and listen to the family, much less time to be still and listen to God and pray.

But even a few minutes alone with God in prayer is better than none. You can pray while driving or waiting in car line or standing in line at the grocery store. Don't let the cares of the world consume your mind so much that you are not able to focus on God and bring Him your prayer requests. Also, as you're rushing around, you could keep a small notebook or an app on your phone to write prayer requests so that you can lay them before the Lord when you get home. Just remember Who gave you your breath and life so that you will lay down your life for Him. When I begin my day in prayer and reading the Bible, I find myself praying without ceasing throughout the day. (1 Thessalonians 5:17) That is the goal.

Guilt from past sin

Adam and Eve hid in the garden after they sinned, and this pattern of hiding sin continued with their descendants. Their sin caused them to stop talking to God, which is what prayer is about.

Satan battles with our minds, hoping to hold us captive to the slavery of worrying and feeling guilty over our past mistakes and sins. But these guilt feelings can cripple us and keeps us leaning on our own understanding rather than leaning on God's understanding. We need to constantly talk to God through prayer so that we don't hold on to guilt and run from Him like Adam and Eve did.

Since the Messiah has come on the scene, though, and died for all of the guilt and sin of the world, those who have put their faith in Him don't have to carry that guilt anymore. God says that once we repent and believe in the provision of eternal life through Christ that our sins are gone "as far as the east is from the west." (Psalm 103:12)

When guilt feelings try to keep you from prayer, you can just turn them on their heads and say, "Thank you, Jesus, that I've been forgiven of those sins!"

Lust

Lustful temptation can arise when two people spend too much time together in work or ministry, especially when one or both of them is married. If this arises, ask God to take away the temptation. If it continues to consume your mind, you can keep going to a prayer place and writing it down over and over again. As you do, keep trusting in the power of Jesus Christ in His victory over sin, to overcome this temptation.

Sometimes a temptation like this can get beyond control. In that case it is essential to "run like Joseph." In Genesis 39, Joseph was a slave, and his master's wife wanted him badly. One day she grabbed Joseph's tunic, and he ran away. Even though she screamed and he ended up in jail for something he never did, God used him for an extraordinary job and worked it all out for good. Joseph always stayed faithful to God through hardships and trials, and we need to do the same.

Cultural distractions

From 24-hour news channels to smartphones, cultural distractions have gotten in the way of not only building our relationships with friends and family, but also spending quality time with God in prayer. Even though social media and movies at the touch of a button can entice us to distractions, it's crucial to make sure we're prioritizing our time for prayer.

I can remember a time when I would go to my prayer closet, shut the door, and my mind would wander to things on my phone like "to do" lists and social media. Pray and ask God to help clear your mind from these cultural distractions so that you can focus on prayer and His word.

 ## Applications

Read Luke 5:1-11.

1. According to Luke 5:1-5, what did Simon Peter do when Jesus said to put his nets down into the water?

2. What was the result of obedience to Christ, noted in Luke 5:6-7?

3. According to Luke 5:8-9, what can happen when we obey and lay down our lives to Christ?

4. According to Luke 5:10, what is the will of God Jesus reveals for our lives once we surrender and lay them down before Him?

5. Do you find this similar to the Shepherd leaving the 99 sheep to find the one lost sheep?

6. In Luke 5:11, what is God's goal for all of us once we receive the gift of salvation?

7. According to John 3:1-9, do you think Nicodemus was hesitant to lay down his life for Christ? How about you?

Actions

Pray for yourself

At your special prayer place, bring the prayer verses from the end of chapter 6 before God. Use these to pray for yourself before praying for others, just as Jesus did in John 17. God will change your heart to become like His instead of the selfish desires you once possessed.

Pray for others

Write down prayer requests for others, including family and friends. Also, add other people who are just acquaintances, who may not know Christ as their Lord and Savior. Lay them down before God in prayer as Hezekiah did when he took the threatening letter to the temple.

This process of laying down prayer requests teaches us to rely on and trust in God. You can lay out before God those life situations that are causing you worry and stress. They may include things like, "What should we do for our adult mentally handicapped daughter? Should we try to keep her at home, or should we put her in a care facility?" or "What about my elderly Dad with Alzheimer's?"

God cares about these pressing issues and wants to help you. Trust Him that He will care for you as His beloved child.

Lay it down and spend more time with God.

CHAPTER 8

Wait

Lamentations 3:25-26 (NKJV)
"The Lord is good to those who wait for Him,
To the soul who seeks Him.
It is good that one should
hope and wait quietly
For the salvation of the Lord."

If you think about "waiting on God" too literally, you can end up with a wrong notion of what it is. It doesn't mean stop everything you're doing and wait for the couch to levitate.

In reality, waiting on God and leaning on His understanding mean to keep living life, but yield as He redirects you.

Examples of being redirected

In the Old Testament, prophets gave warnings to redirect God's people. But the Israelites wandered and strayed from God and the warnings of the prophets, so He allowed their enemies to capture them so that they would acknowledge their wrongdoings.

The message delivered to them was always to repent of their evil ways. Only then would God restore them. Every time and without fail, when God's people repented, God saved them.

In the New Testament, God's Spirit redirected His people. Paul went on mission trips to spread the good news of Jesus Christ, but as he traveled, God's Spirit redirected him to wherever the Lord saw fit.

Paul and the other apostles didn't put out a fleece to test God (the way Gideon did in Judges chapter 6), and they didn't waver in following God's decisions. Instead, they boldly moved forward as He guided them.

Waiting struggles

Every Christmas when I was young, my seven siblings and I opened our presents ahead of time. We got so crafty at re-wrapping and carefully replacing the tape that our parents never noticed. Sometimes even we couldn't tell the gifts were rewrapped!

There's no doubt that waiting can be painful. Our culture will say, "Just do it" and "It's for you."

But God's timing doesn't always line up with ours. To wait on God well, our hearts will desire the things that God desires and we will want to build His kingdom more than our own.

When it comes to things like opening presents, the problem of being unable to wait is usually solved by getting older. But other expectations and hopes can become more difficult to wait for as we age.

What about waiting for a beloved family member to recover from a life-threatening illness? Or long single years waiting for a spouse? Or waiting for an abusive spouse to become kind and loving? Or waiting for financial burdens to be lifted?

Or what about waiting for God to do a work in our own hearts, to change us into the image of Christ that we so deeply desire?

I have had most of these waiting times in my life; not only in ministry but also in my personal life. When my family was moving at one point, we lived with my father for a few months. What was supposed to be about 6 weeks grew into three months. At the time, it seemed like eternity waiting for the house to be finished in another city two hours away and having four young daughters to take care of in someone else's house. I like organization and it just wasn't possible in this circumstance.

While I was there, the time with my father was amazing for my children, making memories for a lifetime.

Once we finally moved, I could see God's hand in the waiting period for moving because my dad suddenly became ill and actually died six months later. I, along with my kids, always treasured their time with Granddaddy. I could see that God's waiting period was actually a gift of a special blessing that I now treasure in my heart.

There are many circumstances in our lives that require waits that seem like they're just too long, but we can turn to God during them to wait for Him to show what He might be doing in the background.

Bible characters who had to wait

Job

Job, a servant of God, endured a painful waiting period during a trial from God when he suffered greatly. Satan brought about severe trials against Job, including the loss of his children and a terrible disease.

This scenario shows us a nearly unbearable time of waiting on God. Job yearned for God to heal his body so he could find rest.

Have you been through a time where you crave for physical health but have to wait? The pain or itching might have been so bad that you couldn't sleep and your body felt like it just wanted to die.

At one point, Job said that it would have been better if he had never been born. Have you ever felt that way? If so, then you are not alone. Some people who follow God are going through times like these daily.

Job faithfully waited on God, and God restored his health and his family. As you trust God and wait on Him, you can be confident that He'll do what's best for you as well.

Abraham

The Lord promised Abram that he would have descendants as numerous as the stars. Later He changed his name to Abraham, meaning "father of many."

In Genesis 15, 75-year-old Abram (Abraham) reminded God that he still didn't have the son God had promised him. But once again the Lord promised him he would have a son, and through that son would have innumerable descendants.

Genesis 15:6 (NKJV) tells us that Abram "believed in the Lord, and He accounted it to him for righteousness."

Abraham followed God closely, but the waiting was excruciating. When his wife, Sarah, thought she was too old to have children, she urged him to take matters into his own hands by having a son with her handmaid.

Sadly, this plan caused much pain and hardship. Abraham wanted to lean on God's understanding, but instead he chose the wrong path.

After enduring these trials and consequences, though, he learned to trust God and wait on Him. In the end, God delivered His promise through Abraham's son Isaac. Through Isaac, Abraham fathered the nations that became as numerous as the stars in the sky just as God promised.

Moses

Moses was called by God to deliver the Israelites out of slavery in Egypt and lead them to the Promised Land "flowing with milk and honey."

A journey that should have taken a few weeks ended up taking 40 years. But throughout the whole time of waiting, Moses fully depended on God's presence. Daily he met with God in his private tent as God's presence came over it in a cloud or fire.

As Moses set an example of waiting and leaning on God's understanding, the people watched in amazement from their tents as the holy and powerful God met with Moses.

Even though the wait was long, Moses still trusted that God would lead His people into the Promised Land. Every step of the way, all 40 years, he still trusted that God would keep His promise. And He did.

Sometimes your wait might seem long too, as you wait for God to answer your desperate plea for help. But you can trust that one day He'll open the door for you and give you the strength to step through it.

While you wait, you can remember that His word will be a comfort for the soul.

What to do while waiting

If you become desperate, tired, and discouraged during your waiting period, you might . . .

- Give up and turn away from God to the idols of the world.

Psalm 139:7-10 says, "Where can I go from Your Spirit? Or where can I flee from Your presence? If I ascend to heaven, You are there; If I make my bed in Sheol, behold, You are there. If I take the wings of the dawn, If I dwell in the remotest parts of the sea, Even there Your hand will lead me, And Your right hand will lay hold of me."

Upon reading the words of the psalmist, you can see that God won't stop pursuing you. The best option is to lean on God's understanding and follow Him. He knows what's best for our lives just like the Shepherd knows what is best for His sheep. He is the only One who truly loves and cares for us.

- Turn to drugs and alcohol that suppress the pain of waiting.

People who choose this option may seem happy for a while, but after some time, their lives often fall apart. They need to be encouraged to keep asking God for help, even though their situations may seem hopeless at times. This is why it's so important that they find other Christians who can comfort and encourage them, to give them a peace to want to follow God more closely. Psalm 20:6 says, "Now I know that the Lord saves His anointed; He will answer him from His holy heaven with the saving strength of His right hand."

If Christians will trust that God's hand is strong enough to handle their problems and hold them up in this world, then they will eventually see Him work in mighty ways.

- Dive so deep into work or hobbies that they become an idol.

Many times, people will avoid following God because they become so occupied with work or hobbies; they give up on waiting on God. Don't get me wrong, it is difficult to wait on God's timing. Most of the time, it takes months and years of waiting for answers to our prayers, but if you keep turning to Him, after time, you see that you have an advocate in Him. When He answers little requests along the way, there is reassurance that He is all powerful and in control. Definitely a God worth waiting for.

- Ask God to teach you during your wait and allow Him to mold you into a person with stronger faith.

Waiting for God to act can be such a trial that we can become impatient, lose faith, and give up on Him. But during those tough waiting periods we can pray Psalm 139:23-24, "Search me, O God, and know my heart; Try me and know my anxious thoughts; And see if there is any hurtful way in me, And lead me in the everlasting way."

If you're open in communication with God during these difficult waiting periods, He will change your heart and mind to allow you to feel His peace while you follow Him. The result is leaning on His understanding while you wait.

Christians are on this earth for only a short time. Jesus will return one day to set up His new Kingdom, where we will live in paradise with no pain, tears, or sorrow.

Keep these promises of blessings in mind as you approach and endure waiting periods in life. Ask God during the struggles of waiting to hold you and uplift you to rise above the pain and allow Him to teach you.

Applications

1. For Whom was John the Baptist waiting in Matthew 3:11-12 when he was preaching in the wilderness of Judea and baptizing those who repented?

2. What struggles of trickery did John the Baptist face in Matthew 3:7 while he waited for Jesus?

3. According to 1 Peter 2:24, what was Jesus waiting to do during His 33 years on earth?

4. In Acts 9:15-16, what was God's future plan for Saul (Paul) when he was blinded by Jesus and waited for 3 days?

5. According to Acts 2:1-6, what were the frightened and powerless disciples and followers of Jesus waiting for?

6. According to Hebrews 10:13, what is Jesus waiting for?

7. What are we instructed to wait for according to Philippians 3:20-21?

Actions

Read and memorize

Read and memorize Bible verses about waiting. Several are listed below, but you can search the word *wait* on a Bible app to find more verses on waiting. Write them on index cards or print them out so that you can read through them before bed or whenever you get a chance.

An excellent way to memorize is to pray verses back to God. Learning these verses will teach you to wait on God. The highlighted verse at the beginning of this chapter will be good to learn also.

- Psalm 25:5 "Lead me in Your truth and teach me, For You are the God of my salvation; For You I wait all the day."
- Psalm 27:14 "Wait for the Lord; Be strong and let your heart take courage; Yes, wait for the Lord!"
- Psalm 33:20 "Our soul waits for the Lord; He is our help and our shield."
- Psalm 40:1 "I waited patiently for the Lord; And He inclined to me and heard my cry."
- Psalm 106:13 "They quickly forgot His works; They did not wait for His counsel."
- Psalm 130:5-6 "I wait for the Lord, my soul does wait, And in His word do I hope. My soul waits for the Lord more than the watchmen for the morning."

- Hosea 12:6 "Therefore, return to your God, Observe kindness and justice, And wait for your God continually."
- Isaiah 25:9 "And it will be said in that day: 'Behold, this is our God for whom we have waited that He might save us. This is the Lord for whom we have waited; Let us rejoice and be glad in His salvation.'"
- Isaiah 40:31 "Yet those who wait for the Lord will gain new strength; They will mount up with wings like eagles, They will run and not get tired, They will walk and not become weary."
- Isaiah 64:4 "For from days of old they have not heard or perceived by ear, Nor has the eye seen a God besides You, Who acts on behalf of the one who waits for Him."

CHAPTER 9

Enemy Attack

Ephesians 6:11-13
"Put on the full armor of God, so that you will be able to
stand firm against the schemes of the devil.
For our struggle is not against flesh and blood,
but against rulers, against the powers,
against the world forces of this darkness,
against the spiritual forces of wickedness
in the heavenly places.
Therefore, take up the full armor of God,
so that you will be able to resist in the evil day,
and having done everything, to stand firm."

When we experience hardships in this world, we might be tempted to think, "Why would God let this happen to me?" But these stresses that so often induce such panic might be indicating that there's a spiritual battle going on. After all, Satan will do everything in his power to keep God's people from following Him.

Once we become saved from sin and death, it is vital to learn to fight our enemy, Satan.

The pattern for spiritual warfare

One of the best guides to fighting the enemy can be found in the Old Testament books of Ezra and Nehemiah. The enemy works more or less the same with everyone, so we can find patterns to his crafty schemes.

We can see Satan's attacks on us displayed through the battles in the Bible and it can help us today. The books of Ezra and Nehemiah describe the rebuilding of God's temple and the rebuilding of the walls of Jerusalem after 70 years of desolation. The enemies of God challenged this rebuilding, and by analyzing the enemy's tactics and actions, we can see how Satan tries to thwart the plans of God in our lives as well.

We can all learn from the four stages of rebuilding in the books of Ezra and Nehemiah, so we can actively rebuild our lives too.

Stage one: Preparations to rebuild

In both Ezra and Nehemiah, there was a spiritual crisis. Seventy years earlier, the enemy nation of Babylon had destroyed Jerusalem, burned the temple, and deported all the inhabitants to captivity in Babylon.

Now it was time to return. God wanted His temple rebuilt so the people could come together and worship Him. This was because His presence rested in the temple at the Most Holy Place.

Be unified

The book of Ezra says that when it came time to return to Jerusalem and rebuild the temple, the men gathered as one man, unified in their efforts, following Biblical guidelines to build altars to God for sacrifices.

Together they followed each specification for building as outlined by the temple blueprints from God's word. It was critical to comply with God's word in rebuilding the temple, and it is crucial to comply with God's word in our lives also.

Be dedicated

The people also reestablished sacrifices and worship to God. As we rebuild our lives that have been harmed by sin and struggles, we need to dedicate our lives to God and worship Him through praise and prayer just as the Israelites did in Ezra's day.

Be determined

The book of Nehemiah describes the walls of Jerusalem, which had fallen into such extreme disrepair that the city was left vulnerable to enemies.

But interferences from enemies meant that rebuilding the walls wasn't as straightforward as it seems like it should have been. The enemy's efforts were so successful that the rebuilding of the temple halted for 15 years.

Finally God moved the pagan king to send Nehemiah from captivity back to Jerusalem. There he led the reconstruction of the walls of Jerusalem for protection.

The preparation was tedious, because the enemy was always present and fighting. But Nehemiah was so determined to succeed that he even conducted his wall inspections at night, to avoid conflict.

In our lives, we need to make preparations to rebuild also. When we go through struggles, God wants us to take steps to pursue and follow Him for direction in the struggles. We can prepare our hearts for His rebuilding by being unified, dedicated, and determined.

Stage two: Rebuilding

Once preparations have been made to rebuild, there are more steps to take.

Power and praise

In Ezra, the workers began sorting through the rubble that used to be the city of Jerusalem. When the enemy had burned Jerusalem to the ground, their goal was to destroy the source of power. But they didn't know that the power of Jerusalem was the presence of God Almighty, who was still helping His people.

As the workers gathered for rebuilding, the priests also gathered for worship and praise. Praise is important for us too, as we are rebuilding our lives in a spiritual crisis. Psalm 18:3 says, "I will call upon the Lord, who is worthy to be praised; And I am saved from my enemies."

Working together

In Nehemiah, the rebuilding of the walls involved going around to all of the gates to recruit workers. The people who lived at each gate gathered their friends and family to work together during the rebuilding.

Nehemiah 3:1-3 shows us how they worked together: "Then Eliashib the high priest arose with his brothers the priests and built the Sheep Gate; they consecrated it and hung its doors. They consecrated the wall to the Tower of the Hundred, and the Tower of Hananel. Next to him the men of Jericho built, and next to them Zaccur the son of Imri built. Now the sons of Hassenaah built the Fish Gate; they laid its beams and hung its doors with its bolts and bars."

The rebuilding was a tedious process because no part of the wall could be left undone. It was important for the people to work together.

Consecration

Another step of the rebuilding involved consecrating the walls, which meant dedicating them and their reconstruction to the glory of God.

As we rebuild our lives to serve and follow God, we can follow this important step of consecration, staying in close communication with God during the entire process.

Stage three: Battles

After you seek God to rebuild your life, you can expect roadblocks and battles presented by the enemy Satan.

In Ezra 4:3 as the Israelites were rebuilding the temple, the enemies came craftily saying that they wanted to help the rebuilding efforts. They claimed that they made sacrifices to God too, so they were also His people and were worthy to help.

But Zerubbabel, the governor of the Israelites, could see through their lies and schemes. He answered them, "You have nothing in common with us in building a house to our God; but we ourselves will together build to the Lord God of Israel, as King Cyrus, the King of Persia has commanded us."

In a case like this, you might think the enemies would give up, but instead, they ruthlessly tried various tactics to weaken the temple builders and frustrate their purpose. They wrote letters to the king of Babylon, urging him to cut off monetary support for rebuilding the temple of God. They made up other malicious lies as well.

The result was that the Israelites gave up, and temple construction was halted for 15 years.

Do you ever feel that way in your Christian walk? Maybe you've experienced grief at work or school for being a Christian, and you feel tempted to quit. Don't give up, because just like the Israelites' faith eventually revived and they overcame their battles, the same can happen to you with God's help.

In the book of Nehemiah, enemies came in a similar way, asking if they could join in on the rebuilding the walls. Again, they wrote divisive letters, five times asking for Nehemiah to be pulled from the building project.

When Nehemiah continued refusing to leave the walls of Jerusalem to talk with them, the enemy said, "They will not know or see until we come among them, kill them and put a stop to the work." (Nehemiah 4:11)

That's what Satan does to us today too. When we try to do God's will, Satan wants to come into our midst and do what I like to phrase "swoop down" to confuse us or fill us with fear. Don't worry about these swooping efforts, though, because God is on your side as Overcomer.

Nehemiah told all the families and workers to hold a sword in one hand as they worked with the other. Many had to stoop down to avoid swooping darts of destruction. To encourage them, Nehemiah did three things:

1. *Prepared their hearts* by saying, "I stationed people in families with their swords, spears, and bows. Do not be afraid of them [the enemy]." (Nehemiah 4:13-14) God put the family together to work for overcoming enemy battles. Keep that in mind if you have stress in your family. Pray for them daily.

2. *Prepared their moves* by telling them how to fight. They needed their armor of weapons, and they needed the armor of

God. Nehemiah 4:17 says, "Those who were rebuilding the wall and those who carried burdens took their load with one hand doing the work and the other holding a weapon."

3. *Encouraged their hearts* by calling the nobles and other people to say, "Remember the Lord, who is great and awesome, and fight for your brothers, your sons, your daughters, your wives, and your houses." (Nehemiah 4:14) The people were so encouraged that they finished the wall in just 52 days.

Stage four: Battles overcome

In Ezra there came a time when the battles ceased and the rebuilding could begin again. This was when two of God's prophets, Haggai and Zechariah, spoke to these wounded, deflated children of God. Haggai said in Haggai 2:4-5, "'But now take courage . . . and work; for I am with you,' declares the Lord of hosts. . . . 'My Spirit is abiding in your midst; do not fear!'"

The Israelites had allowed the enemies to get the best of them, and they forgot to set their mind on God's promises of future peace through the coming Messiah. When they heard the prophet's message, they were encouraged and renewed in purpose of rebuilding for God's glory.

Zechariah was another prophet who added a message of hope, giving the people confidence in God, even though they might not have understood God's ways and why He allowed them to go through such battles. He assured them that God would deliver them from these times of oppression and that the damaging actions of the enemies would cease. His overarching message was that God would one day bring "My servant the Branch" who would establish peace in the world and would exalt Israel once again. (Zechariah 3:8)

The Israelites put their hope in the fact that if the temple were rebuilt, then God would restore their nation. But now with this news from the prophet, they were assured that it would happen. This hope gave them the confidence they needed to press on in the rebuilding efforts.

Today when you're tempted to give up, press on knowing that King Jesus did grace that very temple with His presence when He walked on earth, and one day He will return to set up His new Kingdom. Think about the promise of no pain, no tears, streets of gold, crystal thrones, and the very presence of our Lord.

Enemy tactics

Before learning how to fight the enemy, it's crucial to know how the enemy works, just as football teams and boxers analyze their opponents' strategies.

In Ezra and Nehemiah, Satan used men who were opposed to God, to write letters to hinder the rebuilding efforts. Here are the tactics they used.

Tricks

Enemy letters tricked the king into halting the Israelites' rebuilding for God. How about you? Have you ever received an email, letter, or text that was aimed to trick you? In these instances, do not panic but call on God.

Discouragement

The diabolical efforts of the enemies in the books of Ezra and Nehemiah deflated the workers' morale. In Nehemiah the conflict was so intense, they had to hold a sword in one hand while they rebuilt the walls. When multiple letters falsely accusing the Israelites kept coming to them, their hearts sank.

Have you ever had a sinking heart when you had a right motive, but you were accused falsely of wickedness? Maybe you thought you could trust someone with private information only to find out they twisted your words, and as a result, you were accused falsely. The enemy will try to use this sinking heart feeling of discouragement to stop you from serving God. Seek God's counsel at times like these.

Fear

In Ezra the workers were so afraid that they stopped building the temple, and in Nehemiah the enemy swooped down in efforts to kill them. Fear gripped the Israelite families who worked on the gates and walls.

Today the enemy can frighten you so much that it can tie you in knots. When this happens, remember 2 Timothy 1:7 (NKJV), which says, "For God has not given us a spirit of fear; but of power and of love, and of a sound mind."

Bribes

The enemy tried to bribe Nehemiah constantly, hoping he would leave the workers at the gates and walls alone so they would be vulnerable. Five different times he received letters attempting to lure him away from the task at hand.

The enemy may try to bribe you like he did Nehemiah. We must be on guard at all times against bribery efforts from the enemy.

Frustration

Satan attempted to frustrate the efforts of rebuilding to thwart God's plan. This enemy is ruthless and comes over and over in an attempt to frustrate our efforts for God.

Turn to God, continually knowing that He has the power to overcome these tactics. Write them down and lay the requests before God in prayer.

Overwhelming road blocks

In the book of Ezra, the enemy used force and power to stop the rebuilding efforts of the temple. Being forced to stop building was confusing for the Israelites because they had been commanded to rebuild.

The same type of confusing roadblocks can occur in our lives as we attempt to follow God. Finding mature Christians in a good church family can help you through struggles such as these. Remember the church is not a building, but it is a group of people who belong to God and love God and love and care for others. If you don't have a good church, pray about it and keep searching until you find a loving family of God to protect and care for you.

Enemy identified

It is essential to identify who your enemy is. In Zechariah 3, God gave Zechariah the vision to identify the enemy. The people might have believed their enemy was all the men in Jerusalem causing mayhem, but in reality, the enemy was someone else.

Zechariah's vision showed a scene with Joshua, the high priest, standing before the angel of the Lord, and Satan there standing at his right hand, trying to harm him. Zechariah could see that Satan was the one trying to stop this entire building effort.

We can remember Zechariah's vision when we go through struggles, stresses, and trials. The Bible tells us many things about Satan: 2 Corinthians 4:4 says, "The god of this age has blinded the minds of unbelievers, so they cannot see the light of the gospel that displays the glory of Christ, who is the image of God." And he "disguises himself as an angel of light" (2 Corinthians 11:14) and tricks people into thinking he is the real God.

He also "prowls around like a roaring lion, seeking someone to devour." (1 Peter 5:8)

Ephesians 6:12 says, "For our struggle is not against flesh and blood, but against the rulers, against the powers, against the world forces of this darkness, against spiritual forces of wickedness in the heavenly places."

How to fight the enemy

By the power of God

Zechariah received a message from God saying, "This is the word of the Lord to Zerubbabel saying, 'Not by might nor by power, but by My Spirit.'" (Zechariah 4:6) The Israelites had a history of trying to fight by their power and might, which resulted in panic and calling their surrounding neighbors for military assistance. It wasn't until they gave up and watched God fight the battles that they tasted success and victory. They discovered it was only by God's spirit that they could win victories.

Have you ever been tempted to make things happen by your effort, only to find out you were spinning your wheels? Remember, not by your might or power, but by God's Spirit do things get done successfully.

And remember the most crucial battle that God fought for us: after Jesus' death and burial, He rose again from the dead to bring us eternal life.

With the help of the Holy Spirit

When Nehemiah was rebuilding the wall, a trumpet would sound every time the enemy was sighted. The trumpeter stayed by Nehemiah's side at all times for warning. Today the Holy Spirit does the same for us as our helper. Praise God daily for our helper of the Holy Spirit who gives us warnings and empowers us against our enemy the devil.

With prayer

Nehemiah prayed before doing anything. For example, when the King, whom he served as cup bearer, asked why he looked sad, he prayed before answering. Every step Nehemiah took was bathed in prayer, and we should be doing the same.

With the armor of God

Upon salvation, we acquire God's armor, so we need to know about these tools that we possess for battle.

The Belt of Truth was a metal mesh protection for the loins. Today our truth is God's word. The word tells us that Jesus, God, and Holy Spirit are truth. Study the word to know about truth.

The Breastplate of Righteousness covers the heart, which is most important to God. Upon salvation, we have the righteousness of God that we can depend on. Genesis 15:6 (NKJV) says, "And he (Abraham) believed in the Lord, and He accounted it to him for righteousness."

Feet Shod with Peace is the sure foundation of Christ that we stand on. If we don't have a solid foundation to stand on, it's impossible to fight.

The Shield of Faith also guards our hearts. Use your shield of faith with confidence that Christ died and has already won the battle.

The Helmet of Salvation guards our minds, which the enemy wants to claim. Look at how the enemy frustrated the minds of the exiles rebuilding the Temple, and they stopped for 15 years. Once the prophets came to tell them the words of God, they resumed their work.

The Sword of the Spirit is the word of God. The word is compared to a "two-edged sword" (Hebrews 4:12), which is powerful but can be dangerous if it isn't wielded proficiently.

Read the word of God daily so that you can know it and become proficient. If you find yourself too busy, then listen to the word on a Bible app. Keep the word on the tip of your tongue so that you can use it any time battles arise.

After over 70 years, the end of the book of Nehemiah tells us that Ezra the priest brought out the law of God to read to the people in Jerusalem. Since the Temple had been built and the walls completed, this was a joyous occasion.

Even though the reading of God's word brought conviction of sin and weeping, Ezra told them to go feast and celebrate the goodness of the Lord because "the joy of the Lord is your strength." (Nehemiah 8:10)

This is an important truth to remember when we also face battles like the ones the Israelites faced in the days of Ezra and Nehemiah.

 Applications

Read Matthew 4:1-11.

1. According to Matthew 4:1, who was with Jesus to help Him while He was being tempted?

2. In Nehemiah 4:18-20, what instrument was used to warn the people that represented the Holy Spirit of God?

3. According to Matthew 4:3-4, what trick and bribery did Satan try to use on Jesus?

4. What did Jesus use to fight Satan that was successful according to verse 4?

5. What did Jesus tell Satan that refers to the Word of God in Matthew 4:4?

6. According to Matthew 4:8-9, what did Satan promise to Jesus if He would bow down to him?

7. What was the result of Jesus using the sword or word to fight Satan according to Matthew 4:11?

Actions

Memorize Jesus' words

Memorize the three things Jesus said to Satan to defeat him while being tempted in the wilderness. Use these when you face stresses or mind wandering so that you can learn to lean on God's understanding.

- Matthew 4:4 "It is written, 'Man shall not live by bread alone but on every word that proceeds out of the mouth of God.'"
- Matthew 4:7 "It is written, 'You shall not put the Lord your God to the test.'"
- Matthew 4:10 "Go, Satan! For it is written, 'You shall worship the Lord your God, and serve Him only.'"

CHAPTER 10

Hear My Cries

Psalm 18:6
"In my distress I called upon the Lord,
And cried to my God for help;
He heard my voice out of His temple,
And my cry for help before Him came into His ears."

David's distress in this psalm came because he desperately wanted help. Crying out for help in times of need is natural, almost like an automatic response when we're faced with danger or uncertainty.

Just as a woman whose purse has been stolen will cry out for help, stressful times can cause us to cry out for help to God. C.S. Lewis, a famous Christian apologist, said, "Pain is our megaphone."

God's desire to teach us wisdom

When we cry out for help from God, He wants our hearts and attention to lean on Him, and He will begin to give us His wisdom. Psalm 51:6 (ESV) says, "Behold, you delight in truth in the inward being, and you teach me wisdom in the secret heart."

The "secret heart" in this verse seems to refer to the part of our heart that we cling to the most. If you have a place in your heart that you're keeping from God, whether it's because of sin or shame, you can know that when you finally do offer it to Him, He'll lovingly receive it and fill it with His wisdom.

When we cry out for help, we might be crying the wrong request. Or God might want us to wait for a while because the best option that will bless us the most needs to come a little later.

The world says, "Go get it now" but God says, "Wait and give me all of your life and emotions" until you get answers.

The example of Joseph

In the book of Genesis, Joseph had plenty of reasons to cry out to God for help, because he was an innocent man who was forced into slavery and then imprisoned.

Joseph was one of the youngest of the 12 sons of Israel. His father favored him, giving him a coat of many colors, which made his brothers jealous. Their jealousy led them to sell Joseph into a life of slavery in Egypt.

Many people would want to die if this happened to them, but Joseph continued to turn to God and serve Him throughout this horrible experience.

In Potiphar's house

As a slave, Joseph was sold to the wealthy and powerful Egyptian officer Potiphar. He worked diligently and honestly during this time, to the point that Potiphar appointed him as overseer of his house and all he owned.

God blessed everything Joseph touched. Genesis 39:2a says, "The Lord was with Joseph, so he became a successful man."

Joseph couldn't see the end result that God had in mind for his life at the time, and it doesn't seem like a blessing to be a slave. But after all of Joseph's struggles, God had specific plans. Let's keep looking into his life to see them.

In Pharaoh's prison

When Joseph was serving in Potiphar's house, the wife of his master noticed that he "was handsome in form and appearance" (Genesis 39:6b), so she pursued him with the desire to commit adultery with him. He finally told her, "There is no one greater in this house than I, and he [Potiphar] has withheld nothing from me except you, because you are his wife. How then could I do this great evil and sin against God?" (Genesis 39:9)

One day Potiphar's wife tried to force herself on Joseph, but he ran from her. She then began to scream, frantically claiming that Joseph had forced himself upon her.

Because of the false accusations, Joseph was cast into Pharaoh's prison. This was a devastating turn of events. But Joseph knew he had represented God rightfully, so he always stayed hopeful for God's blessings upon his life.

And God did bless him in that prison. Genesis 39:21-22 says, "But the Lord was with Joseph and extended kindness to him, and gave him favor in the sight of the chief jailer. The chief jailer committed to Joseph's charge all the prisoners who were in jail; so that whatever was done there, he was responsible for it."

We can imagine that Joseph must have cried out day after day for God's deliverance from that terrible prison. In hind-

sight, though, as we read ahead in the Bible, we can see that
Joseph was able to bear his difficult experiences because of
God's favor.

We need to keep an attitude like Joseph when we cry out
in our desperation. Remember that Proverbs 3 says to trust in
the Lord. That is God's ultimate goal in our lives, for us to
trust Him and know Him intimately. We cannot trust God until we learn to lean on His understanding and not our own.
Joseph couldn't see what God was doing, but he trusted Him
nonetheless.

Dream interpreter

Joseph had the unusual gift from God of being able to interpret dreams. While in prison, he interpreted the dreams of
two prisoners who had been two of Pharaoh's servants. The
baker told his dream, and Joseph saw that he would, sure
enough, lose his position. Then the cupbearer explained his
dream, and Joseph saw that he would be restored.

Joseph begged the cupbearer to ask Pharaoh for his release, yet the cupbearer forgot about him for two more years,
until the Pharaoh had a frightening dream that no one could
interpret. That dream triggered the cupbearer to remember.

Joseph was brought before the Pharaoh, and showing no
sign of weakness or lack of confidence, he said in Genesis
41:28, "God has shown to Pharaoh what He is about to do."
After seven years of plenty, the land would experience seven
years of famine. God gave Joseph a master plan for a solution.

In Genesis 41:33-36 Joseph said, "Now let Pharaoh look
for a man discerning and wise, and set him over the land of
Egypt. Let Pharaoh take action to appoint overseers in charge
of the land, and let him exact a fifth of the produce of the land
of Egypt in the seven years of abundance. Then let them gath-

er all the food of these good years that are coming, and store up the grain for food in the cities under Pharaoh's authority, and let them guard it. Let the food become a reserve for the land for seven years of famine which will occur in the land of Egypt, so that the land will not perish during the famine."

Pharaoh decided that there was no man more discerning or wise than Joseph, and he appointed him second in command and head of operations.

Look how God delivered Joseph. Not only did He deliver him out of the prison, but He made him one of the highest in the land. Joseph now had the power to save not only the residents of Egypt but also all people in the surrounding regions who would be desperate for help in this time of need.

Joseph did indeed trust God, and because of this trust, God handled the situation in a way no one would have ever dreamed.

We must keep following God no matter how bad our circumstances become. God can do impossible things that we cannot even imagine.

Saving Israel

As the seven years of plenty progressed before the famine, Joseph married, had children, and lived a beautiful life full of blessings. During these plentiful years, he crafted an intricate system for tracking food supplies for the future.

When the famine finally arrived and the surrounding nations were starving, because of Joseph's careful planning, Egypt still had grain.

Among the thousands of people who went to buy grain were Joseph's brothers. The brothers didn't recognize Joseph, but he recognized them. After many tests to humble his brothers, Joseph finally revealed himself to them. Then Joseph, the one who had been sold into slavery and had spent years in prison because of his brothers, embraced them and forgave them.

Then he said in Genesis 50:20, "As for you, you meant evil against me, but God meant it for good in order to bring about this present result, to preserve many people alive."

Joseph could now see what God's intentions had been all along; the suffering he had endured for years had a purpose that he could see. God had used all those trials to grow Joseph in the strength of the Lord so he could be God's representative on earth for salvation of God's people, the Israelites.

As you cry to the Lord for your desires to be met, it helps to reflect on the struggles of people like Joseph. As Joseph was patient in trials and struggles that cause stress, we can pray, "God teach me through this trial and struggle so that I can know what you want me to learn and do for You, similar to Joseph's life." Many times I find myself praying God's words back to Him, and it always seems to help. It is always advantageous to search the Bible for God's answers.

Cry Out To God

Cry out to God freely

After you become a believer, when things go awry in your life you don't need to fret, worry, or get stressed. According to James 1:2-4, troubles are to be expected. "Consider it all joy, my brethren, when you encounter various trials, knowing that the testing of your faith produces endurance. And let endurance have its perfect result, that you may be perfect and complete, lacking in nothing."

As you struggle, you can reflect on the life of Joseph and look ahead to the miracle God carried out through his life.

Ask God to use your life for His glory and do His will through your life. Sometimes you may have to endure trials in order for God to prepare you for the work He has for you.

When I've had enormous trials, after much praying, searching scripture and crying out to God, I get to the point of picturing myself being held in God's hand. That brings comfort and peace in times of turmoil.

If you feel the same way, remember that you're not alone, and the Lord is with you. Also, if you can find good Christian brothers and sisters through these hard times, that will be an extra special blessing.

Hear God's words

God's word to us is full of declarations of His love for us. It also shows us His will for us, that we will want to receive and keep in order to receive His full blessings. His moral will is designed to protect us from harm and danger in our lives, and His providential will that Jesus the Messiah will return to take His church and establish a new heaven and new earth are comforting thoughts and truths to hold on to.

Regarding His moral will, these days for both men and women, it's challenging to live life without sexual temptation. But when provocative images of the world blindside you, you can "run like Joseph" in your mind. Otherwise, sin can take up residence in your mind, crippling you spiritually and bleeding out to affect others.

Joseph did the wise thing and ran away from Potiphar's wife to avoid sin, and we need to run with our minds and hearts, which is where Satan tries to birth sin. Instead of trying to justify the pleasure of sin, you can "run like Joseph" and switch to praying for yourself, praising God, and reciting Bible verses you have memorized.

If you commit to "run like Joseph" when faced with temptation, God will hear your cries and honor your actions.

Keep pure thoughts

Worries, stresses, and temptations can overwhelm our thoughts. But instead, you can think upon good and pleasant thoughts as Philippians 4:4,8 tells us to do: "Rejoice in the Lord always; be anxious for nothing, but in everything by prayer and supplication with thanksgiving let your requests be made known to God. And the peace of God, which surpasses all comprehension, will guard your hearts and your minds in Christ Jesus. Finally, brethren, whatever is true, whatever is honorable, whatever is right, whatever is pure, whatever is lovely, whatever is of good repute, if there is any excellence and if anything worthy of praise, dwell on these things."

Run in your mind to the peace of God instead of to the stresses, worries, and temptations of daily life.

Resist Satan's calls

Satan speaks into our ears at all times, either loudly or in seductive whispers. But James 4:7 says, "Submit therefore to God. Resist the devil, and he will flee from you."

When you watch a parade at the street, you can see only one part at a time. But God can see the parade from above, below, front, back, around the corner, and even down the street ahead of them.

God sees our lives the same as that parade. He knows all and is all, so we must trust in Him alone. He will guide and direct us in our daily lives. He is the only One who can hear our cries and solve them for us. He is worthy of our trust.

Joseph found out the hard way that he couldn't trust his brothers, Potiphar's wife, or the cupbearer. But over those years, Joseph learned beyond a doubt that he could always trust God.

Joseph experienced disappointment after disappointment, but God never left his side. Instead, all those "disappointments" were used as steppingstones in the process of making a plan to save His people. Joseph genuinely submitted to God even in times of unbelievable stress and struggle. No matter how deep the pain or how awful the struggle, we can also trust God, submit to His word, and follow Him.

Don't give up

In Joseph's life you can see how God used trials to shape him and accomplish His will. He allowed Joseph to become a slave and then a prisoner, only to develop and strengthen him and lead him along His plan to save the lives of many people.

Maybe God is doing something in your life that you don't understand. You can trust Him that through it He is strengthening you for a job He wants you to accomplish for Him. Don't lose heart in the trial but keep seeking God's guidance. We can have the same attitude as Joseph, the same attitude that caused Jesus to cry out to His Father shortly before His death, "not My will but Yours be done." (Luke 22:42)

This is the attitude we must adopt in our lives, to trust God and lean on His understanding. He knows what is best for us, and sometimes that looks quite different from the way we think it should look. Even through our toughest trials, when God is working behind the scenes, it will be better in the end. (Romans 8:28) We can turn to Him through each stress and dilemma and ask Him to carry us through them.

Satan wants us to lean on our own understanding instead of God's. But looking at the life of Joseph from the bird's-eye view can give us hope in our grueling situations. When Satan cries in your ears to give up, you can keep turning to God.

Don't let disappointments in life change your faith in God, because He will never leave you or forsake you.

 Applications

Read Ephesians 1.

1. Even in the midst of trials and stresses, what blessings does God wish for all believers, according to Ephesians 1:3?

2. According to Ephesians 1:7, what does God's grace provide for us that is more important to Him than our comfort levels with stresses and trials?

3. According to Ephesians 1:9, what is God trying to make known to us in our lives?

4. According to Ephesians 1:17, what is God's goal for Christians to gain and know?

5. What does God want us to see with the "eyes of our heart," according to Ephesians 1:18-19?

6. According to Ephesians 1:22-23, Who is head over the church?

7. According to 1 Peter 1:3-9, what proves our faith? (see verse 7)

 ## Actions

Cry out to God

One way to give words to your cries is by going to a Bible program such as www.biblegateway.com and entering words that describe your cries. An example might be *sadness* or *sad.* Then you can look up the verses that are recommended and copy the ones that mean a lot to you. Put them in your prayer place, asking God to take your struggles.

At one point in my struggles, I looked up 2-3 words every day. After reading all that God had to say about my struggles, I was amazed to understand more about Him. It's like going to a counselor, but the counselor is God.

In the next chapter, you'll learn another exercise that will help you turn your cares over to God even more.

CHAPTER 11

The Last Straw

Isaiah 53:4
"Surely our griefs He Himself bore
And our sorrows He carried;
Yet we ourselves esteemed Him stricken,
Smitten of God, and afflicted."

When you learn to cry out to God but still find yourself stuck with the problem, that's when you reach your last straw. But it's essential to hang tight, because He's worth the wait.

Satan's goal is always to knock us down, but remember that "God causes all things to work together for good to those who love God." (Romans 8:28)

For example, suppose you and your spouse need to sell your house, but the market is upside down.

Or worse, you've been suffering from a disease for which there is no known cure. In situations like these, God could have a different plan for you.

Whatever the case, you can ask God to help you lean on His understanding so you won't fret. Psalm 37:8-9 says, "Cease from anger, and forsake wrath; Do not fret; it leads only to evildoing. For evildoers will be cut off, But those who wait for the Lord, they will inherit the land."

The example of Jesus

Beginning of time

After Adam and Eve sinned, in Genesis 3:15 God said to Satan, "And I will put enmity between you and the woman, And between your seed and her seed; He shall bruise you on the head, And you shall bruise Him on the heel."

The bruising of Christ's heel took place through His death on the cross, and then the crushing of Satan's head took place in His resurrection that brought victory, destroying Satan's havoc of sin.

Humble birth

Jesus, the true King, deserved to be born in a palace, not a stable; in a royal crib, not a manger; greeted by kings, not lowly shepherds. Luke 2:7 says, "And she gave birth to her firstborn son, and she wrapped Him in cloths, and laid Him in a manger, because there was no room for them in the inn."

Jesus was born to be the King of the Jews, but nobody recognized Him as King. John 1:11 says, "He came to His own, and those who were His own did not receive Him."

This is because He came to be a servant and not a proud, wealthy king like Solomon. Jesus never demanded the kind of treatment a true king should expect, because His humble heart came to serve others. Luke 19:10 says, "For the Son of Man has come to seek and to save that which was lost."

Though Jesus was rejected when He was on earth, one day every knee will bow to Him. Philippians 2:10-11 says, "at the name of Jesus every knee should bow, of those who are in heaven and on earth and under the earth, and that every tongue will confess that Jesus Christ is Lord, to the glory of God the Father."

Wretched temptation

Jesus had to endure more hardships than any man who lived on earth. One of His greatest hardships occurred when He was called away into the wilderness after His baptism. He fasted and prayed for 40 days and nights to prepare for His ministry, and then Satan came in order to tempt Jesus.

Jesus had to fight this enemy. He fought with the word of God from the Old Testament, and ultimately His steadfastness caused Satan to flee.

Jesus endured trials such as these, trusting God through them. We can follow His example throughout life, in all of our challenging experiences, leaning on God's understanding.

The apostle Paul followed Jesus' example of leaning on God's understanding through challenging trials. He wanted to show people how to be saved from sin and death so they could have eternal life through Jesus Christ. In Acts 20:18-22, he said to the Ephesian church, "You yourselves know, from the first day that I set foot in Asia, how I was with you the whole time, serving the Lord with all humility and with tears and with trials which came upon me through the plots of the Jews; how I did not shrink from declaring to you anything that was profitable, and teaching you publicly and from house to house, solemnly testifying to both Jews and Greeks of repentance toward God and faith in our Lord Jesus Christ. And now, behold, bound in the Spirit, I am on my way to Jerusalem, not knowing what will happen to me there."

Paul leaned on God's understanding for the furtherance of the gospel so that people could believe and have eternal life.

When you get wrapped up in your problems, think about the fact that one day we will leave this earth and be in our true home with our heavenly Father. Ask God if He has a particular job for you during your time on earth. Sometimes our struggles arise to get our attention so we will come to God for answers and direction.

Living on earth

While on earth, Jesus endured stresses and trials like the ones we experience, and worse. In order to save humankind from sin and death, He had to live a human life. Hebrews 4:15 says, "For we do not have a high priest who cannot sympathize with our weaknesses, but One who has been tempted in all things as we are, yet without sin."

Jesus, our high priest, experienced temptations in life just as we do today, but He had no sin and always leaned on God the Father's understanding.

As a human, Jesus sometimes needed to escape from the crowds who surrounded Him so that He could be alone with God the Father. Even though Jesus was God, He had human feelings on earth, so He leaned on God's understanding to deal with the human stresses He had to experience.

For us, we may think we have reasons to complain to God about our stresses in life, but Jesus went through even more for us. Make sure to always take your problems to God in prayer and ask Him to guide you in proper steps to solve the issues. Write them down, give them to God and then turn to likeminded Christians at church for brainstorming resolutions.

It helps to keep your focus on glorifying God in your life. Jesus brought glory to the Father at all times, even if things were terrible. God desires that we follow Jesus' example as to how we are to live and act on earth.

Challenged by earthly authorities

The leaders of the Jews conspired against Jesus and falsely accused Him left and right, because they felt that their positions of power were threatened by His popularity. After Jesus spoke claiming He was God and predicting His death, He said to the disciples in Matthew 26:2, "You know that after two days the Passover is coming, and the Son of Man is to be handed over for crucifixion." This scripture goes on to say, "Then the chief priests and the elders of the people were gathered together in the court of the high priest, named Caiaphas; and they plotted together to seize Jesus by stealth and kill Him. But they were saying, 'Not during the festival, otherwise a riot might occur among the people.'"

Because of His intimate connection with God while on earth, Jesus was aware of the schemes of these leaders. But He also knew His promised destiny and purpose. He stayed calm and collected through all the drama.

The traitorous disciple Judas also schemed with the chief priests and elders to have soldiers arrest Jesus. Matthew 26:47-50 says, "Judas, one of the twelve, came up accompanied by a large crowd with swords and clubs, who came from the chief priests and elders of the people. Now he who was betraying Him gave them a sign, saying, 'Whomever I kiss, He is the One; seize Him.' Immediately, Judas went to Jesus and said, 'Hail, Rabbi!' and kissed Him. And Jesus said to him, 'Friend, do what you have come for.' Then they came and laid hands on Jesus and seized Him."

Did it bother Jesus that one of His disciples turned on Him in hopes of gaining money for His death? Many of us would fight back, demand respect, run away, or freeze out of fear, but not Jesus.

This saga of the attempted defeat of Jesus continued when the chief priests, elders, and counsel in Matthew 26:59 "kept trying to obtain false testimony against Jesus, so that they might put Him to death." Then in verse 60-61 two false witnesses came forward and said, "This man stated, 'I am able to destroy the temple of God and to rebuild it in three days.'"

Even with all these attacks, Jesus reacted in the best way possible. After the high priest accused Him of blasphemy, He simply stayed silent. Even in the midst of these storms of life, He remained peaceful, but His actions spoke a multitude of wisdom.

The only way that peace can be possible in life's storms is by leaning on God's understanding.

Once when Jesus did speak in John 8:44, He exposed Satan's work in the lives of the Jewish leaders, saying, "You are of your father the devil, and you want to do the desires of your father. He was a murderer from the beginning and does not stand in the truth because there is no truth in him. Whenever he speaks a lie, he speaks from his own nature, for he is a liar and the father of lies."

Jesus calmly exposed Satan's lies with His words. We can also use the word of God today, to expose Satan as he tries to destroy us.

The road to Calvary

Matthew 27:27 says soldiers "stripped [Jesus] and put a scarlet robe" on Him, which made a mockery of this Holy King deserving of worship.

Matthew 27:29 says "And after twisting a crown of thorns, they put it on His head, and a reed in His right hand; and they knelt down before Him and mocked Him, saying, "Hail King of the Jews!"

In Matthew 27:30, they "spat on Him, and took the reed and began to beat Him on the head." Matthew 27:31 adds that they "took His robe and put His clothes back on and led Him to be crucified."

In Matthew 27:34-37 "they gave Him wine to drink mixed with gall, and after tasting it, He was unwilling to drink. And when they had crucified Him, they divided up His garments among themselves by casting lots. And sitting down, they began to keep watch over Him there. And above His head they put up the charge against Him which read, 'This is Jesus King of the Jews.'"

Probably the most degrading action was when passers-by blasphemed saying, "You who are going to destroy the temple and rebuild it in three days, save Yourself! If you are the Son of God, come down from the cross." (Matthew 27:40)

"In the same way the chief priests also, along with the scribes and elders, were mocking Him and saying, "He saved others; He cannot save Himself. He is the King of Israel; let Him now come down from the cross, and we will believe in Him. He trusts in God; let God rescue Him now, if He delights in Him; for He said, 'I am the Son of God.'" (Matthew 27:41-43)

Have you ever been falsely accused? Maybe you only wanted to make things right, but every attempt was twisted into another accusation. False accusations are what Jesus kept experiencing, but He was not panicked, because He knew His destiny, and He knew that on the other side of the cross "joy [was] set before Him." (Hebrews 12:2) He would be seated at the right hand of the throne of God.

What an act of love! John 3:16 says, "For God so loved the world, that He gave His only begotten Son, that whoever believes in Him shall not perish, but have eternal life." If you were in Jesus' shoes on the road to Calvary, what would you have done? Would you have had a temper tantrum? Would you have begged for help? Would you have fallen to the ground and lain there?

Instead of doing any of these, Jesus was calm, with rock-solid faith in His Father. He leaned on God's understanding through all of His stressful persecutions and trials. We can do the same.

 Applications

Read Matthew 5:1-12.

1. According to Matthew 5:3-5, what blessings will we receive if we are poor in spirit, mourning over sin, and meek?

2. What happens if we hunger and thirst for righteousness, according to Matthew 5:6?

3. What is the reward for being a pure in heart peacemaker, according to Matthew 5:8-9?

4. According to Matthew 26:55-56, what was Jesus' reaction when one of His followers betrayed Him? How does He want us to react in similar situations?

5. According to Matthew 27:11-14, how did Jesus react when He was falsely accused?

6. According to Matthew 5:11-12, why did Jesus act so calm during His persecutions?

7. According to Philippians 2:5-8, Whose attitude should we have in our spiritual walk?

 ## Actions

Problem exercise

If you went to a counselor, you would be told to describe your problem and your feelings about it. That's exactly what you'll do in this exercise, with God as your Counselor. The great thing about God being your counselor is that He is there to listen to your problems 24/7.

Before you begin, make sure to pray and ask God to direct this exercise. Allow Him to be your counselor through it.

First, you can make 2 or 3 columns on paper or on the computer. Then write a description of your problem. It could take three sentences or a full page or more.

Then write two words that describe how you feel about this problem.

Then write one word describing what you want God to be in this situation (for example, *Provider, Healer, Husband, Shepherd,* or *Master*).

Then look up all three words (for example, *frustrated, sad, Provider*) in a Bible concordance or a Bible program such as www.biblegateway.com to find several verses that may apply to your situation. Copy the verses you find about the three words you've looked up.

Once the exercise is done, lay the sheets out before God in prayer. Let Him know what you're going through and ask for Him to do His will. Then trust God to direct you on how to handle the issue.

Here is an example.

YOUR NAME	GOD	JOB
Describe what you want in a future job. For instance, job security, more time with family, more money to give to the needy. Write your feelings and frustrations on paper as if you were sitting with a counselor.	Write what you think God would want for your future workplace. For instance, a job that would allow you to pay the bills while spending more time with God and your family and more time showing His love to others.	Describe a job you're seeking. Maybe ask for a less stressful environment at work than your current or past job. Ask for favor on the interviews and that your decisions would be made in God's will.

Possible words to describe how you feel about the situation:

Frustrated
Isaiah 14:27 - "For the Lord of hosts has planned, and who can frustrate it? And as for His stretched-out hand, who can turn it back?"

Your prayer with this verse might be for God to clear the way for you to get a job that will provide for your family.

Sad

Proverbs 15:13 - "A joyful heart makes a cheerful face, But when the heart is sad, the spirit is broken."

Your prayer with this verse might be for God to heal your spirit by providing a job where you can spread joy to others.

Possible word to describe what you want God to be in this situation:

Provider

Psalm 147:8 - "Who covers the heavens with clouds, Who provides rain for the earth, Who makes grass to grow on the mountains."

Your prayer with this verse might be since God provides for the earth, He will surely provide for you.

The key to the Problem Exercise is that through His word God will give you knowledge, understanding, and wisdom to handle decisions.

This exercise can be used for many different types of life struggles, such as job searches, relationships, and health struggles. Choose God as your counselor and go to Him with all your life needs. He may want you to ask friends, family, and church for help, but go to Him first.

CHAPTER 12

Gain Strength

Philippians 4:13
"I can do all things through Him
who strengthens me."

Stresses and trials can push us to cry out to God and seek Him. When we seek Him through the Bible, we can develop understanding and wisdom that leads to trusting Him more. As we trust Him more and more, we can rely more heavily on His strength, finding that, in time, it becomes our own.

First Corinthians 1:25b says, "the weakness of God is stronger than men." It's important to know more about how to gain that strength from God.

Gaining physical strength

Gaining muscle from lifting weights or working out isn't a once-and-done affair. You can't walk into a gym, lift a dumbbell 200 times, and then gain all the muscles you want.

Instead, the trainer would most likely stop you and advise an alternate plan of working out. He'd probably suggest starting with even-set reps over time to train the muscles and then change up the sets to wake up the neurological system, which ignites muscle mass.

Getting into shape also depends on developing a healthful diet, getting the right amount of sleep, and undertaking other aspects of a healthful lifestyle in order to see a significant change in overall body image.

Similarly, most of the time people don't become amazing Christians and strong warriors for God overnight, but they must practice specific "training" actions over a long period of time.

So what are some examples of Bible people who struggled and then gained God-given strength in the process?

The people of Israel

Before the era of the kings, the Israelites rebelled against God time and time again, so He appointed judges to convict them of their sin and rescue them. In Judges 6, the oppression, hardships and ultimate captivity got the attention of God's people. This caused them to reflect on their sin and thus repent.

The Israelites went through four phases in the process of growing closer to God through hardships, thus gaining strength in the long run.

Turning from God

During the time of the Judges, the Israelites over and over again refused to follow God and ran away from Him. For their own good, God allowed them to be defeated by pagan nations so they could reflect on their sins and repent. For example, Judges 6:1 says, "The sons of Israel did what was evil in the sight of the Lord, and the Lord gave them into the hands of Midian."

Do you ever refuse to do things God's way and end up in a bind? If you turn to God, then things can change. God is a merciful God and will always allow you a way to repent and follow Him wholeheartedly.

Oppression

Because the Israelites turned to the gods of their neighbors, God let them find out what it was like to ask those gods for help. Judges 6:2 says, "The power of Midian prevailed against Israel." Evil nations oppressed Israel by destroying crops, land, and animals, and even sometimes taking their people captive. The destruction forced the Israelites to flee to the mountains for safety. Judges 6:6a says, "Israel was brought low because of Midian."

Have you ever been brought to what you would call your lowest point in life and found God was the only One strong enough to bring you out of it?

Crying out

Judges 6:6b continues, saying, "the sons of Israel cried to the Lord." At that point, God sent a prophet to the Israelites to give them a wake-up call. In Judges 6:8b-10, God told them, "It was I who brought you up from Egypt and brought you out from the house of slavery. I delivered you from the hands of the Egyptians and from the hands of all your oppressors, and dispossessed them before you and gave you their land, and I said to you, "I am the Lord your God; you shall not fear the gods of the Amorites in whose land you live. But you have not obeyed Me.""

The Israelites had continued to turn away from God as the only One worthy to be followed, and now they were forced to face the consequences of sin. They needed to acknowledge the supremacy of God and their need to repent. They needed to recognize that it was wiser to follow God and His ways than the neighbors' gods and their ways.

Similar outcomes can occur with us today when we drift from God. When we feel oppressed, we need to remember to cry out to God and recognize His strength.

God's rescue through Gideon

The book of Judges tells us that God raised up Gideon to save the people of Israel. Judges 6:12b-13 tells us that an angel said to him, "The Lord is with you, O valiant warrior." Gideon replied, "O my Lord, if the Lord is with us, why then has all this happened to us? And where are all His miracles which our fathers told us about, saying, 'Did not the Lord bring us up from Egypt?' But now the Lord has abandoned us and given us into the hand of Midian."

Gideon doubted his worth for the use of God in defeating this enemy. But God assured him in Judges 6:16, saying, "Surely I will be with you, and you shall defeat Midian as one man."

Victory in weakness would seem impossible for any of us to imagine, but once we learn how God dealt with people in the Bible, we can understand His ways more and trust Him.

Judges 7:12 says, "Now the Midianites and the Amalekites and all the sons of the east were lying in the valley as numerous as locusts; and their camels were without number, as numerous as the sand on the seashore."

Gideon thought he would need a huge army against this vast enemy, but in the end, God defeated the powerful Midianite armies with only 300 men. He told Gideon to divide the 300 men into three groups of 100, who blew trumpets and shouted, "A sword for the Lord and for Gideon!" (Judges

7:20b) All the enemy armies fled as fast as they could to get away from the small army of Israel.

There was no question that God won this battle, and thus He received all the glory. After witnessing the strength and power of God, the hope and faith of the people of Israel were restored.

In our lives, we need to turn to God and believe that the impossible is possible with Him, so that our faith in God's strength and power will grow.

Samson

God called Samson to fight against the Philistines who had been oppressing His people for 40 years. Samson's proud and willful heart made life more difficult for him while he served God as one of the judges of Israel. Several things contributed to his fall.

Lustful relationship

Samson came to his parents, saying, "I saw a woman in Timnah, one of the daughters of the Philistines."(Judges 14:2) Even though she was of the enemy nation, because he lusted after her, he begged his parents to allow him to take her as his wife.

This relationship was out of bounds when it came to God's will, and Samson knew it.

Have you ever ached for a relationship with someone who was "out of bounds"? Perhaps they weren't right for you, and deep down you knew they were hazardous to your future. Whatever the case, you may be able to relate to Samson's feelings, but there are consequences to going outside of God's boundaries.

Samson's consequences were very hazardous, and he lost this lustful relationship in the end.

Pride

Samson possessed a great gift from God: extraordinary strength to defeat the Philistines. But he became prideful about his gift of physical strength and frivolously used it to pursue two other women.

One of these women, Delilah, was approached by the Philistines to help them destroy Samson. After many tricks and fights, he finally gave up the secret to his strength, which was his hair. The consequence was that the Philistines captured and blinded him.

Pride is a significant way the enemy attacks. Pride can bring terrible consequences, including irresponsible behavior, so it's crucial that we turn our minds away from ourselves and toward the Lord. Satan used this tactic with Samson, and he uses it on us today.

Pride was also one of the three temptations Satan used to tempt Jesus in the wilderness. Satan promised Him the world and all of its glitz and glory if Jesus would only bow down to him. But Jesus replied in Luke 4:8, "It is written, 'You shall worship the Lord your God and serve Him only.'"

The way of obedience

For Samson, it took the loss of his strength and imprisonment for him to finally learn to obey God.

During a celebration to their gods, the Philistines brought Samson out, to mock him. But he prayed for strength one last time, to push the pillars apart, which would destroy the temple, the enemies of God . . . and himself.

God granted Samson's request.

Samson's end was death, but God allowed him to save his people by destroying the powerful Philistines. His pride led to his fall, but God's will was still accomplished.

If we surrender to God's will and follow Him, then we can do great things for Him without harmful consequences like Samson.

Joshua

While the Israelites were on the journey to the Promised Land, Joshua led them in a battle against the enemy nation of Amalek. Moses told Joshua that Aaron and Hur would be on the top of the hill with him to support his battle efforts through prayer.

Exodus 17:11-12 says, "So it came about when Moses held his hand up, that Israel prevailed, and when he let his hand down, Amalek prevailed. But Moses' hands were heavy. They took a stone and put it under him, and he sat on it; and Aaron and Hur supported his hands, one on one side and one on the other. Thus his hands were steady until the sun set."

This battle can remind us to pray to ask God for His guidance and strength.

Maybe when you've gone through a hardship, you've had likeminded Christians standing alongside you through your stress and struggles. They can refer you to select Bible verses and remind you of God's love and strength when you're too weary to read the Bible yourself. They can "support your hands" in prayer.

Sometimes God allows our weakness so He can offer us His strength and love through others.

John and Peter

In Acts 3:1-10, Peter and John healed a man who had been lame from birth. People were amazed to see this man "walking and praising God."

But Peter was quick to give the glory for this healing to God and not to himself and John. He began preaching to the people right there, saying, "Men of Israel, why are you amazed at this, or why do you gaze at us, as if by our own power or piety we had made him walk? The God of Abraham, Isaac, and Jacob, the God of our fathers, has glorified His servant Jesus, the one whom you delivered and disowned in the presence of Pilate, when he had decided to release Him. But you disowned the Holy and Righteous One and asked for a murderer to be granted to you, but put to death the Prince of Life, the one whom God raised from the dead, a fact to which we are witnesses. And on the basis of faith in His name, it is the name of Jesus which has strengthened this man whom you see and know; and the faith which comes through Him has given him this perfect health in the presence of you all." (Acts 3:12-16)

Leaning on God caused strength to arise in these men. Later after being flogged and imprisoned for their preaching, Peter and John gathered the other Christians and prayed, "O Lord, it is You who made the heaven and earth and the sea, and all that is in them, who by the Holy Spirit, through the mouth of our father David Your servant said, 'Why did the Gentiles rage, and the peoples devise futile things?'" (Acts 4:24b-25)

Seeing this Old Testament scripture prophesied about their experience caused them to feel confidence, strength, and peace in the midst of their trial.

Acts 4:31 says, "And when they had prayed, the place where they had gathered together was shaken, and they were filled with the Holy Spirit and began to speak the word of God with boldness."

These servants of God made sure that everyone knew it was only by God's strength that they could heal a man, preach the gospel with boldness, or do anything at all for God.

Paul

The apostle Paul had been so wicked that he had ordered Christians to be tortured for their faith in Christ. But on the road to Damascus, Jesus struck him down with blindness, and Paul's life was transformed.

The experience of going blind for three days convinced Paul that he was nothing and he needed to rely on God's strength alone. God had to knock this prideful man down so that He could use him for His glory.

Towards the end of his life and ministry, after writing much of the New Testament, Paul said in 2 Corinthians 12:7-10, "Because of the surpassing greatness of the revelations, for this reason, to keep me from exalting myself, there was given me a thorn in the flesh, a messenger of Satan to torment me—to keep me from exalting myself! Concerning this I implored the Lord three times that it might leave me. And He has said to me," My grace is sufficient for you, for power is perfected in weakness". Most gladly, therefore, I will rather boast about my weaknesses, so that the power of Christ may dwell in me. Therefore I am well content with weaknesses, with insults, with distresses, with persecutions, with difficulties, for Christ's sake; for when I am weak, then I am strong."

Paul's words beautifully sum up the concept of gaining strength in Christ. Following God and leaning on His understanding will result in gaining strength in Christ.

A life of following God might not always make sense, but it is the most rewarding way to live. There were many times in Paul's life when he did not understand what God was up to, so he always prayed and surrendered before God. Paul's life is a great example for us.

What we can learn from these examples

Gideon

Gideon gained strength by depending on God's wisdom. He thought he needed to gather a vast army to achieve victory against his enemies. But when a tiny army of 300 achieved the victory, he saw the display of God's perfect strength. God's strength is always enough in our lives also.

Samson

Samson's pride blocked his submission to God. He gained the most strength by repenting of sinful pride and submitting to the Lord's power. Pray that God would reveal any pride in your life, repent of it, and turn to God.

Joshua

In the battle against the Amalekites, Joshua gained strength from God as other like-minded believers prayed for him. Ask God to surround you with other Christians to lift you in prayer.

Peter and John

God gave Peter and John strength through persecution. They rejoiced while being persecuted, which is the example

Jesus displayed for them during His ministry. Pray that you will be able to rejoice during times of persecution.

Paul

Paul gained strength through understanding his weakness. Our weakness reminds us that our strength comes only from the Lord and not through our efforts.

If we keep focusing on God and His word, we'll see His strength and gain hope while following Him. In Matthew 28:20b Jesus said, "I am with you always, even to the end of the age." If we obey Him by faith in our weakness, then He will use us and make us strong through His strength, not our own.

 # Applications

1. According to Hebrews 11:32-34, what made these men and prophets go from weakness to be made strong? (See verse 33.)

2. According to Hebrews 12:12-14, what are believers commanded to do for the weak?

3. According to Romans 15:1, what are the strong in Christ commanded to do?

4. According to 1 Corinthians 1:26-27, what has God done with weak and strong things?

5. According to 1 Corinthians 10:22, who is stronger than we are?

6. According to Psalm 24:8, who is the source of strength?

7. According to Philippians 4:12-13, in what way does God make us strong?

 ## Actions

Pray

Ask God to give you His strength not your own.

Pursue like-minded Christians

Ask other likeminded Christians to pray for you so that you will gain strength in your pursuit to walk with God and lean on His understanding.

Memorize and learn verses

Memorize and learn the following strength verses and look up other strength verses in a concordance or on a Bible program such as www.biblegateway.com.

GAIN STRENGTH • 149

- Psalm 28:7 "The Lord is my strength and my shield; My heart trusts in Him, and I am helped; Therefore my heart exults, And with my song I shall thank Him."
- Psalm 31:2 "Incline Your ear to me, rescue me quickly; Be to me a rock of strength, A stronghold to save me."
- Psalm 37:39 "But the salvation of the righteous is from the Lord; He is their strength in time of trouble."
- Psalm 59:16 "But as for me, I shall sing of Your strength; Yes, I shall joyfully sing of Your lovingkindness in the morning, for You have been my stronghold and a refuge in the day of my distress."
- Isaiah 11:2 "The Spirit of the Lord will rest on Him, the spirit of wisdom and understanding, the spirit of counsel and strength, the spirit of knowledge and the fear of the Lord."
- Isaiah 40:29 "He gives strength to the weary, And to him who lacks might He increases power."
- Isaiah 41:10 "Do not fear, for I am with you; Do not anxiously look about you, for I am your God. I will strengthen you, surely I will help you, Surely I will uphold you with My righteous right hand."
- Isaiah 58:11 "And the Lord will continually guide you, And satisfy your desire in scorched places, And give strength to your bones; And you will be like a watered garden, And like a spring of water whose waters do not fail."
- First Peter 4:11 "Whoever speaks, is to do so as one who is speaking the utterances of God; whoever serves is to do so as one who is serving by the strength which God supplies; so that in all things God may be glorified through

Jesus Christ, to whom belongs the glory and dominion forever and ever. Amen."

- 1 Peter 5:10 "After you have suffered for a little while, the God of all grace, who called you to His eternal glory in Christ, will Himself perfect, confirm, strengthen, and establish you."

CHAPTER 13

Loneliness

Matthew 14:23
"After he had sent the
crowds away, He went up
on the mountain by Himself to pray:
when it was evening.
He was there alone."

Jesus spoke parables of wisdom to the unbelieving crowds, but most of them didn't care to understand His words and wisdom, and found little value in them. To find comfort and strength, Jesus often got alone with God the Father so He could get a taste of heaven on earth.

When we fully devote our lives to the Lord, we can feel that other people don't understand us. That can make us feel lonely. But in times like this, God doesn't want us to worry and fret. The wisest decision in situations like these is to get alone with God as Jesus did and saturate yourself with His words.

Elijah's lonely place

The prophets of God in the Old Testament were often most likely very lonely, because they were called by God to wake up the Israelites to repent, and usually the Israelites didn't want to listen.

For example, God called the prophet Elijah to announce to wicked King Ahab and Queen Jezebel that there would be a famine in the land that would cripple their kingdom. Then, after telling them about the famine, Elijah found to his surprise that God called him to sit by a secluded brook, to be alone *for over a year and a half.*

God's goal at the brook was to train and prepare Elijah for the challenges to come in his ministry.

Do you face challenges and wonder what God is up to at times? Do you rest in Him while you learn?

In his loneliness, God provided

God sent ravens to deliver food to Elijah while he waited at the brook. Ravens are notorious for stealing food in crafty ways, fighting over it, and eating it "ravenously," so it was clear that God was in control of this miracle.

When God showed Elijah His power through using wild animals, Elijah experienced His provision. He sensed God's presence and knew he was not really alone at the brook.

Do you stay close to God and talk to Him? He wants you to experience His provision also.

In his loneliness, God protected him

Many people wanted Elijah dead, including wicked Queen Jezebel, who would have had him killed if he had stayed in Samaria. Though Elijah escaped the horrors of Jezebel and her idols, he later received word that she had killed all of the other prophets of God remaining in Samaria. Out of fear, some of the remnant of believers who were left in Samaria bowed down to Jezebel's idols.

Psalm 1:1-2 says, "How blessed is the man who does not walk in the counsel of the wicked, Nor stand in the path of sinners, Nor sit in the seat of scoffers! But his delight is in the law of the Lord, And in His law he meditates day and night."

There was no godly counsel anywhere in Samaria, so God gave Elijah His protective godly counsel every day at the brook.

In his loneliness, God prepared him

God wanted Elijah to "be still and know God," as Psalm 46:10 (NKJV) says, "Be still, and know that I am God. I will be exalted among the nations, I will be exalted in the earth!"

At this quiet brook, Elijah could be still, learn to trust God, and learn patience. Even though Elijah was alone, he learned to be content with God's direction, thus leaning on God's understanding, not his own.

God might be taking you to a quiet place like the brook, to shape you and help you understand what His goals in life are for you. He may allow you to be alone so that He can teach you the way He taught Elijah.

Don't fret if you suddenly find yourself alone; turn to God for help and guidance.

In his loneliness, God reassured him

While God was preparing and teaching Elijah at the brook, He reassured him every step of the way. As a result, after his time alone, Elijah left the brook prepared to do mighty works for God.

After he came back to Samaria, Elijah went to a mountain, where he gathered all 850 pagan prophets and all the Israelites on a mountain. There he called on God, who rained down fire from heaven that licked up the altar and twelve barrels of water that had drenched it.

Through this miracle everyone could see God's power, so the Israelites bowed down to the living God, and the pagan prophets were put to death.

Elijah saw that waiting over a year and being alone with God was worth the time.

In your own life, you may not understand how being still with God and reading His word is beneficial, but rest assured God has a plan. Like Elijah, you can keep seeking God and His word when you feel lonely, trusting that one day He will strengthen you do to great things for Him.

Are you lonely?

Do you find yourself feeling lonely in a crowd?

When you're not around likeminded people, you can pray for anyone in the crowd who might not know Jesus as their Savior. You'll be surprised at the joy you can experience when you pray for the welfare of others, and maybe God will bring someone out of the crowd who is a Christian, or someone for you to share His good news of salvation.

Do you find yourself feeling lonely in your city?

Sometimes big cities can be the loneliest places on earth.

People in big cities can seem like they're on the go all the time, juggling careers, family events, and other activities. The result can be stress, anger, and a general alone feeling.

When I lived in a larger city, I felt this way, so I specifically prayed about it. Surprisingly, the answer to my prayer was to move back to my home town.

Don't forget to present your loneliness to God to see what He wants for your life.

Do you find yourself feeling bouts of loneliness each day?

When bouts of loneliness hit, seek God to ask Him if He is trying to teach you something similar to the experience Elijah had while he sat alone by a secluded brook. Instead of wallowing in your loneliness, you can take action by calling on God for help. He wants to be your joy in life, and you can spend more time with Him. Read or listen to the Bible for comfort.

Do you feel lonely at work?

Sometimes at work, decisions are made that don't include you. You might become disheartened and feel lonely. Don't let these feelings consume you, but take them to God. Chances are He will direct you to pray for these coworkers.

Do you feel lonely at home?

This can be especially hard if you live alone or in a dysfunctional relationship. Home is a place where you should feel loved and adored.

But you can take your loneliness to God and let Him teach you, filling your mind and heart with His promises of hope and love.

Turning to God will safeguard against temptations and sin, like what King David experienced when he was bored and went out on his rooftop to see Bathsheba bathing. This one act of boredom led to sin that caused consequences that deeply affected David's life.

Do you ever feel like you're the only person in the world going through a particular struggle?

It's natural to feel as if we're the only person in the world going through dark and difficult circumstances.

But in reality, no matter how great their lives might look on social media, most people are going through their own problems too. That's why there are divorce groups, recovery groups, grief groups, parent groups, and other kinds of groups, so that people can get the help they need with others and know they're not alone.

Knowing that you're not alone will in itself lighten your load. You can gaze at the stars at night, knowing that many other people in the world are going through similar struggles.

This is one reason it's important to turn to God's word, because you'll see so many people in the Bible who go through feelings and sorrows similar to yours, trusting God for help.

Defeating Satan's goal

Satan's goal is to keep us alone so that we won't be able to encourage others.

When Queen Jezebel ordered Elijah's death, he ran a hundred miles away and then sat all alone under a juniper tree and asked God to kill him. If Elijah had stayed in this discouragement, he could never have done all that God had intended for him in his ministry.

Ultimately, though, Satan's goals for Elijah were defeated. He went on to train up Elisha, who did more miracles for God than any other prophet. Elijah was taken up to heaven in a chariot of fire and was present at Jesus' Transfiguration. In spite of his discouragement, Elijah was an overcomer.

The same applies to us today. Satan wants us to stay alone and depressed. God's will is for us to know Him deeply and then share the good news of salvation through Christ whenever we can. Satan hates this fact and continually tries to block us from sharing this good news.

Jesus said in Matthew 5:13-15, "You are the salt of the earth; but if the salt becomes tasteless, how shall it become salty again? It is no longer good for anything, except to be thrown out and trampled by men. You are the light of the world. A city set on a hill cannot be hidden; nor does anyone light a lamp and put it under a basket, but on a lampstand, and it gives light to all who are in the house. Let your light shine before men in such a way that they may see your good works, and glorify your Father in heaven."

Jesus wants us to fight the enemy's temptation to hide away all alone. He wants us to shine to others around us. We are a reflection of Christ and must seek His guidance so that we can represent Him well.

A cure for loneliness

Get alone with God.
Read about God's assurance for you.
Write down prayer requests.
Focus on praising God.
Listen to the Bible.
Memorize the Bible.
Experience joy in Christ.
Lay your requests at the foot of the cross.

When I feel lonely, the best way to cure it is to get alone with God. I know He will never leave me or forsake me. Hebrews 13:5b refers to Jesus' words in saying, "being content with what you have; for He Himself has said, 'I will never desert you nor will I ever forsake you.'"

This truth is so reassuring, knowing that God is with you and you are not alone. If you get in the habit of writing down prayer requests and leaving them at your prayer place, it will become easier to let go of the stresses and problems that weigh down your mind. This way, your mind's focus can be on praising God, listening to and memorizing the Bible, and feeling joy in Christ, while realizing you are being directed and guided. Lay your requests at the foot of the cross where Jesus died for all of our sins.

Our loneliness many times causes us to feel weak so that God can become strong in our lives. Second Corinthians 12:9a sums it up, "My grace is sufficient for you: for power is perfected in weakness."

Weakness and loneliness, along with trials and disappointments, can be used by God to develop and strengthen us for His work, so don't give up while facing them.

Upon becoming a Christian, it is important to seek like-minded people through a church or group activities. Bible study groups are also helpful for overcoming lonely times. Many times, they spur your appetite for the word of God.

You can also go to God's word for answers to any fears or addictions that may have arisen from loneliness. You can search the Bible for words such as *fear* or *lonely* to see what God has to say about them.

Thank God for creating you and giving you breath and life. If you stop to look, you'll be able to see many things to be thankful for. Remembering what God has done for you will give you a better perspective about life.

Recently, I was faced with a loneliness that I had never experienced. After all of my four children had left for college and life, I was all alone. I was faced with a decision of what I was going to do with my life at that time: Would I become sad and wallow in my sorrow? Or would I dive into God's word and seek His counsel? I dove into God's word and found out that He wanted me all to Himself. Within several weeks, I began feeling pushed to write this book, which prayerfully will help others in their walk with the Lord.

This loneliness caused me to turn to God and get to know Him better, so I could truly say that my loneliness was a gift. I pray that you will dive into God's word to give yourself a chance to see if you can be blessed in your loneliness.

Always lean on His understanding and learn to trust Him as you go through lonely times in life.

 Applications

1. According to Psalm 139:14, what is your reassurance that God knows everything about you including your lonely times?

2. According to 1 Peter 5:7, how are you convinced that God wants to know about your anxiety that contributes to loneliness?

3. According to Numbers 11:11 and 15, what other prophet shared similar feelings to Elijah while he was under the juniper tree?

4. According to Ephesians 6:10-12, who was battling against Elijah in addition to Jezebel that caused his discouragement?

5. According 1 Kings 19:13, what did God ask Elijah when he ran for his life from Jezebel? Do you want God to ask you that question concerning your own fears and loneliness?

6. According to Psalm 115:11-12, why should we never feel alone?

7. According to John 5:30, what example did Jesus demonstrate to us about God's will and what we should seek in life?

 Actions

Memorize

Revelation 4:8b (NKJV) "Holy, holy, holy Lord God Almighty, Who was and is and is to come."

Quote this powerful verse whenever you feel lonely, sad, or afraid. This will be sung in heaven at the throne of God, as we praise Him. This verse reveals that Jesus is God who was at the beginning of time, is today seated at the right hand of God the Father, and will return to set up His new Kingdom and defeat Satan once and for all.

.

CHAPTER 14

What Will It Take?

1 Corinthians 15:4-7
"He was buried, and that He was raised on the third
day according to the Scriptures,
and that He appeared to Cephas, then to the twelve.
After that He appeared to more than five hundred brethren
at one time, most of whom remain until now,
but some have fallen asleep; then He appeared to James,
then to all the apostles."

What will it take for you to believe God and follow Him wholeheartedly?

You might think that relying on your own efforts is good enough.

Maybe your life has always gone smoothly, and thinking of following God wholeheartedly feels like it might cause undesired effort or struggle.

Whatever the case, God wants you to look through His lenses to see your world the way it truly is. He wants you to turn to Him and believe in His powerful authority.

He knows what is best for our lives and wants to have a real companionship with us.

Do you have any real companions? The ones who are faithful through thick and thin? Relationships can come and go, but companions are for life, and they get you like none other, your thoughts, your feelings, your passions, and even what makes you tick. You might say that they see you through your lenses.

God wants us to see through His lenses so we can be companions with Him, with a two-way system of communication. For that to happen, we must keep seeking God.

God shows us what He wants us to know about Him through His word. He reveals it to us as we read or listen with an open heart, through the power of His Holy Spirit.

Jeremiah 17:10a emphasizes, "I, the Lord, search the heart." Though God possesses full knowledge of our mind, heart, and soul, He urges us to get to know Him, because He is the One who loves our hearts the most.

The life, death, and resurrection of Jesus show us a glimpse of God's heart of love and power. Jesus went so far as to offer us forgiveness of sins so that we could live forever with God. That is truly a loving God.

Knowing about this sacrificial act of grace is a beautiful reason to follow God wholeheartedly. Once you begin to learn God's Word, you can lean on God's understanding so that you can live in harmony with a clear vision of Christ, seeing through God's lenses.

Some people in the Bible fought against seeing through God's lenses. Once God showed them the truth, they finally gave in to His direction, realizing it was best.

WHAT WILL IT TAKE? • 165

If God had sat down with these people, He may have asked them, "What will it take for you to see through My lenses and finally trust Me?"

Elisha's servant

The prophet Elisha, who had been trained by Elijah, did incredible miracles and deeds, furthering God's Kingdom.

At one point in 2 Kings 6:15b-16, the king of Syria was coming to battle against Israel. Elisha's servant couldn't understand why Elisha remained calm with such a threat on the horizon. His servant said, "Alas, my master! What shall we do?"

Elisha confidently answered, "Do not fear, for those who are with us are more than those who are with them."

Elisha's servant couldn't understand how he could be so trusting of God. Second Kings 6:17 continues, "Elisha prayed and said, 'O Lord, I pray, open his eyes that he may see.' And then the Lord opened the servant's eyes and he saw; and behold, the mountain was full of horses and chariots of fire all around Elisha."

Once Elisha prayed, God opened the eyes of his servant to see why Elisha trusted God so much. At that point, his servant was able to trust God and lean on God's understanding too.

Have you seen God work in other people's lives, and it grew your faith and trust?

Father of demon-possessed boy

In Mark 9:17-24, the father of a demon-possessed boy was having trouble trusting God. If you've ever had a child who was dreadfully diseased or sick, you can probably relate to this man in his reactions to his encounter with Jesus.

He said, "Teacher, I brought You my son, possessed with a spirit which makes him mute; and whenever it seizes him, it slams him to the ground and he foams at the mouth, and grinds his teeth and stiffens out. I told Your disciples to cast it out, and they could not do it."

Jesus replied, "O unbelieving generation, how long shall I be with you? How long shall I put up with you? Bring him to Me!"

The passage goes on to say, "They brought the boy to Him [Jesus]. When he saw Him, immediately the spirit threw him into a convulsion, and falling to the ground, he began rolling around and foaming at the mouth. And He asked his father, 'How long has this been happening to him?' And he said, 'From childhood. It has often thrown him both into the fire and into the water to destroy him. But if You can do anything, take pity on us and help us!' And Jesus said to him, 'If You can? All things are possible to him who believes.' Immediately the boy's father cried out and said. 'I do believe; help my unbelief.'"

What would it take for the boy's father to believe? After years of facing disappointment after disappointment, the boy's father wanted to see the evidence of change with his own eyes.

Jesus proved to him that He was the only way that the boy would be healed, and the father saw and believed.

When you face disappointments that cause your spirit to feel hopeless, you can ask God to help you with your unbelief.

Life is full of struggle after struggle after struggle, but when you trust Him, with all of these struggles will come blessings in disguise that God has planned for you in advance.

The prodigal son

In Luke 15 Jesus told a story about a wealthy man with two sons. One of his sons didn't trust him when it came to making wise decisions.

The prodigal son's father had a plan that would make his son successful. But one problem the son faced was greed: though he should have found trust in his father's decision to wait for his inheritance, he wanted it *now*.

Here is the result of how running ahead of his father's plans led this son down the wrong path. In Luke 15:11-24, it becomes evident.

"A man had two sons. The younger of them said to his father, 'Father, give me the share of the estate that falls to me.' So he divided his wealth between them. And not many days later, the younger son gathered everything together and went on a journey into a distant country, and there he squandered his estate with loose living. Now when he had spent everything, a severe famine occurred in that country, and he began to be impoverished. So he went and hired himself out to one of the citizens of that country, and he sent him into his fields to feed swine. And he would have gladly filled his stomach with the pods that the swine were eating, and no one was giving anything to him. But when he came to his senses, he said, 'How many of my father's hired men have more than enough bread, but I am dying here with hunger! I will get up and go to my father and will say to him, "Father, I have sinned against heaven, and in your sight; I am no longer worthy to be called your son; make me as one of your hired men."' So he got up and came to his father. But while he was still a long way off, his father saw him and felt compassion for him, and ran and embraced him and kissed him. And the son said to him, 'Father, I have sinned against heaven and in your sight; I am no longer worthy to be called your son.' But the father said to his slaves, 'Quickly bring out the best robe and put it on him, and put a ring on his hand and sandals on his feet; and bring the fattened calf, kill it, and let us eat and celebrate; for this son of mine was dead and has come to life again; he was lost and has been found.' And they began to celebrate."

This parable that Jesus presented to the people made it evident that even when you're impatient and decide not to wait on God and follow Him wholeheartedly, He will be forgiving and receive you back to Himself.

If you wait too long, though, your sin will consume your heart. For the prodigal son, it took squandering his inheritance for him to see the light and turn to God wholeheartedly,

Doubting Thomas

After Jesus rose from the dead, many followers witnessed this incredible supernatural event, but many who did not see it were doubtful, including Thomas. He remained skeptical of the news that Jesus was raised from the dead so he said in John 20:25b, "Unless I see in His hands the imprint of the nails, and put my finger into the place of the nails, and put my hand into His side, I will not believe."

The passage in John 20:26 goes on to say, "After eight days His disciples were again inside, and Thomas with them. Jesus came, the doors having been shut, and stood in their midst and said, 'Peace be with you.' Then He said to Thomas, 'Reach here with your finger, and see My hands; and reach here your hand and put it into My side; and do not be unbelieving, but believing.' Thomas answered and said to Him,

'My Lord and my God!' Jesus said to him, 'Because you have seen Me, have you believed? Blessed are they who did not see, and yet believed.'"

Some people today are like Thomas. They say that they won't believe in a God they can't see or touch. But if they would look at the evidence and ask questions, then they could see that the evidence is very powerful.

There are so many evidences of Jesus' miracles and His death and especially His resurrection. Take time to look at all that God said and did in His word.

Paul

The apostle Paul's experience that caused him to believe in Jesus was quite extraordinary and caused an exploding in church growth at that time.

Previously, Paul was having Christians mocked, arrested, and thrown in jail for their faith. This was an evil man who every believer in Christ feared.

But one day on the road to Damascus, Jesus appeared to Paul and blinded him for three days. Once the scales of blindness were removed from his eyes, Paul had a clear vision from God. He knew Jesus was really the Messiah. He could finally see through God's lenses.

Acts 9:3b-6 says, "Suddenly a light from heaven flashed around him; and he fell to the ground and heard a voice saying to him, 'Saul, Saul, why are you persecuting Me?' And he said, 'Who are You, Lord?' And He said, 'I am Jesus whom you are persecuting, but get up and enter the city, and it will be told you what to do.'"

Many people today are like Paul, refusing even to acknowledge God. What will it take for them to surrender to and follow God?

Once you embark on your path with God, He'll begin to teach you how to lean on His understanding. In this, you'll have the assurance that you will never go through struggles alone.

James

John 7:5 says about Jesus, "For not even His brothers were believing in Him." That's why Jesus said in Mark 6:4, "A prophet is not without honor except in his hometown and among his own relatives and in his own household."

James, who eventually wrote the book of James, was one of these brothers of Jesus who didn't believe Him.

What finally changed his mind? The resurrection of Christ.

Once he saw Jesus resurrected, James believed that He was God Himself, and his attitude changed. First Corinthians 15:3b-8 reviews what happened after Jesus rose from the dead.

"Christ died for our sins according to the Scriptures, and that He was buried, and that He was raised on the third day according to the Scriptures, and that He appeared to Cephas, then to the twelve. After that, He appeared to more than five hundred brethren at one time, most of whom remain until now, but some have fallen asleep; then He was appeared to James, then to all the apostles."

James went so far as to call himself a "bondservant of God and the Lord Jesus Christ" (James 1:1), and Acts 15 tells us that he went on to become an overseeing pastor of the church in Jerusalem.

WHAT WILL IT TAKE? • 171

Once he knew about the resurrection, James became humble and leaned on God's understanding. Knowing that even Jesus' unbelieving brother changed his views should make skeptics stop and think about who they are following. Is it an idol, or will they believe in the true God of the universe? Pray for them to know the truth and believe in Christ.

Jeremiah

Maybe you suddenly lost your job, or someone in your life is sick with a terminal disease. These types of stressors and having the rug pulled out from under you can rock your world so much that you may sometimes feel like saying, "God, I am finished with You!"

The prophet Jeremiah is an excellent example of one who might have wanted to give up on God when facing overwhelming stress and trials.

Jeremiah was chained up in a cage for the entire city to view, thrown in a cistern to die, dragged through streets, and finally thrown into prison, all because of his faithful preaching for God.

In Jeremiah 20:7-9 he reached a low point. "O Lord, you have deceived me and I was deceived; You have overcome me and prevailed. I have become a laughingstock all day long; Everyone mocks me. For each time I speak, I cry aloud; I proclaim violence and destruction, Because for me the word of the Lord has resulted In reproach and derision all day long. But if I say, 'I will not remember Him or speak anymore in His name,' then in my heart it becomes like a burning fire shut up in my bones; And I am weary of holding it in, And I cannot endure it."

If you ever feel like Jeremiah, stop to remember who gave you your life and breath, knowing that this sovereign Lord of the universe actually loves you. Spend time focusing on God, remembering His love for you.

He might be protecting you in your struggle or He might even have something better around the corner.

Surely He wants to use this difficult circumstance in your life to help you focus on things of eternal value.

Don't give up on God, but keep praising Him daily, remembering who He is and what He has done for you. Exodus 15:2 expresses this truth saying, "The Lord is my strength and song, And He has become my salvation; This is my God, and I will praise Him."

Jeremiah was a great example for us because he had such a burning fire for God that he couldn't stop speaking for Him, even when he was locked up in prison.

James never believed that his brother was God in the flesh, until he saw His resurrected body. That is what it took for James to know Jesus as his Savior and God. He also knew that His brother was true and cared enough to die for him.

Upon understanding that Jesus died for their sins and had the power to rise from the dead, over 500 followers knew what it would take for them to believe and have faith in the risen Lord and Messiah.

After believing, they felt loved enough to spread to the world the message of Christ crucified, buried, and resurrected. Their new lenses allowed them to see the truth and be set free from sin and death.

What will it take for you to catch fire?

Applications

1. In Mark 1:14-15, why does God want people to surrender and follow Him?

2. According to 1 Corinthians 1:9, what is the compelling reason to trust in God?

3. In Mark 15:32, what did these people say it would take for them to see through God's lenses and believe?

4. According to Psalm 146:8, how does God help people see through His lenses? What does He do once we submit and bow to Him?

5. In the examples of the earlier sections in this chapter like Paul, James, and others, who would you say that you are most like in your current situation in life?

6. In Jeremiah 20:7-9, did he claim to be stronger than God? Do you sometimes feel stronger and more sufficient than God?

7. In Revelation 3:17-19, what does God say to people who feel like they have it all together and don't need Him?

 ## Actions

Pray

Pray Mark 9:24b that says, "I do believe; help my unbelief." Pray this in stressful times and when you're tempted to trust in yourself instead of God. Admit to God when you're having trouble trusting in Him.

That way He can help you believe and grow closer in your walk with Him, and you can also become His companion.

Now He can transform your mind to follow Him more closely.

CHAPTER 15

Transform Your Mind

Romans 12:2
"And do not be conformed to this world,
but be transformed by the renewing of your mind,
so that you may prove what the will of God is, that
which is good and acceptable and perfect."

Learning to lean on God's understanding and not our own understanding involves growing the fruit of the Spirit. The fruit of the Spirit, which is one fruit, not many fruits, consists of love, joy, peace, patience, kindness, gentleness, and self-control. Before a believer can grow this fruit, there are steps that God takes to teach us.

Understand Atonement and Covenant

Atonement for sins is not accomplished by any of our own efforts, but is provided by God alone.

In the Old Testament, the priests had to make sacrifices of all types to follow God's strict instructions for atonement from sins. God operated this way so that all the people would know that it was He who forgave their sins, and it was not by their own deeds or efforts.

There is no way we could pay for our iniquities, but Jesus shed His blood to pay for our sins.

Jesus fulfilled the requirements of the New Covenant, according to Romans 11:26b-27. "The Deliverer [Jesus] will come from Zion, He will remove ungodliness from Jacob. This is My covenant with them, When I take away their sins."

Jacob represents God's people, the Israelites, who would spread the good news of salvation to the world.

Here are some of the covenants God made with His people before the coming of Jesus:

1. His promise to Noah never to flood the earth.

2. His promise to Abraham for protection and blessing offspring as numerous as the stars in the heavens. (Circumcision was a sign of this covenant.)

3. His promise to the Israelites that if they kept the law they would be blessed.

4. His promise of the line of the Messiah through David.

Once we repent and our sins are forgiven, God establishes His New Covenant with us.

Old Covenant to New Covenant

Hebrews 8:7-12 sums up the meaning of the transition from Old Covenant to New Covenant. "For if that first covenant had been faultless, there would have been no occasion sought for a second. For finding fault with them, He says, 'Behold, days are coming, says the Lord, When I will effect a new covenant with the house of Israel and with the house of Judah; Not like the covenant which I made with their fathers on the day when I took them by the hand to lead them out of the land of Egypt; For they did not continue in My covenant,

And I did not care for them,' says the Lord. 'For this is the covenant that I will make with the house of Israel after those days,' says the Lord: 'I will put My laws into their minds, And I will write them on their hearts. And I will be their God, and they shall be My people. And they shall not teach everyone his fellow citizen, and everyone his brother, saying, "Know the Lord," For all will know Me, From the least to the greatest of them. For I will be merciful to their iniquities, And I will remember their sins no more.'"

When we understand the covenant promises of God, our hope and trust in God will grow due to His love and desire for eternal fellowship with us. Realizing God's love and desire will give us the incentive to lean on His understanding, which, according to Proverbs 3:5, is necessary for trust.

It says, "Trust in the Lord with all your heart And do not lean on your own understanding." If we don't lean on God's understanding, we aren't trusting Him.

Does your mind sometimes drift into a tailspin of leaning on your own understanding? Keep reading to find out how this can change.

Understand sanctification

I recall being a new Christian and hearing people at my church say, "Now that you've been saved, you have to be sanctified." I was so confused and went to the Bible to understand what that meant.

After you have received Jesus Christ as your Savior, which forms a covenant with God, sanctification begins, which means He cleanses us and makes us more and more like Jesus.

Hebrews 10:10 says, "we have been sanctified through the offering of the body of Jesus Christ once for all."

Sanctification is God's will, according to 1 Thessalonians 4:3-7, "For this is the will of God, your sanctification: that you should abstain from sexual immorality; that each of you should know how to possess his own vessel in sanctification and honor, not in lustful passion, like the Gentiles who do not know God; and that no man transgress and defraud his brother in this matter because the Lord is the avenger in all these things, just as we all told you before and solemnly warned you. For God has not called us for the purpose of impurity, but in sanctification."

Receiving the Holy Spirit

God's Holy Spirit sanctifies, according to 1 Corinthians 6:11, "but you were washed, but you were sanctified, but you were justified in the name of the Lord Jesus Christ and in the Spirit of our God." With the help of God's Holy Spirit, who is ours upon salvation, believers become sanctified.

Receiving the Word of God

The Word of God sanctifies, according to John 17:17, "Sanctify them by Your truth. Your word is truth."

This scripture reminds us of how we should be reading God's word daily.

Following God's will

Seeking to follow God wholeheartedly means being open to following the will of God. Are you open to understanding what God's will is and following it wholeheartedly? The blessings of God that result from following Him are endless and rewarding.

Understand God's goal in sanctification

How will our lives look different as God is sanctifying us?

Becoming a slave to righteousness

God's goal is that we go from being a slave to sin to a slave to righteousness. Romans 6:19b speaks about this goal. "For just as you presented your members as slaves to impurity and to lawlessness, resulting in further lawlessness, so now present your members as slaves to righteousness, resulting in sanctification."

Romans 6:22 expounds on this goal. "But now having been freed from sin and enslaved to God, you derive your benefit, resulting in sanctification, and the outcome, eternal life."

Growing in wisdom and righteousness

God's goal is that we be in Christ Jesus to gain wisdom, righteousness, and sanctification, according to First Corinthians 1:30. "But by His doing you are in Christ Jesus, who became to us wisdom from God, and righteousness, and sanctification, and redemption."

Gaining self-control

God's goal is that we possess self-control, to avoid lust and sin. First Thessalonians 4:4-5 points to this goal: "That each of you should know how to possess his own vessel in sanctification and honor, not in lustful passion, like the Gentiles who do not know God."

Believing in Truth

God's goal is that we believe in the Truth of God, not the lies of the enemy. Second Thessalonians 2:13 expresses this goal: "But we should always give thanks to God for you, brethren beloved by the Lord, because God has chosen you from the beginning for salvation through sanctification by the Spirit and faith in the truth."

The Truth is the Word of God, which transforms our minds. This Truth takes us to a place where we are no longer a slave to sin but a slave to God. As our minds begin the transformation, we start possessing wisdom and righteousness in Christ Jesus, and we believe this Truth that we are reading in the Bible. God's Holy Spirit reveals all of these truths to our minds, thus transforming our mind.

Producing the fruit of the Spirit

As God continues sanctifying His people, we grow the fruit of the Spirit. In order to grow fruit, the soil first has to be tilled and sometimes even burned for ideal conditions. God does the same "tilling" and "burning" with His children, to grow fruit in them. This process can be uncomfortable, but the final result is spectacular and is a sweet aroma to God at His throne.

Here are some scriptures concerning each part of the fruit:

1. Love

First John 2:5 "But whoever keeps His word, in him the love of God has truly been perfected. By this we know that we are in Him; the one who says he abides in Him ought himself to walk in the same manner He walked."

2. Joy

Hebrews 12:2 "Fixing our eyes on Jesus, the author and perfecter of faith, who for the joy set before Him endured the cross, despising the shame, and has sat down at the right hand of the throne of God."

3. Peace

In John 14:27 Jesus says, "Peace I leave with you; My peace I give to you; not as the world gives do I give to you. Do not let your heart be troubled, nor let it be fearful."

4. Patience

Ecclesiastes 7:8 "The end of a matter is better than its beginning; Patience of spirit is better than haughtiness of spirit."

5. Kindness

Ephesians 2:5-7 "Even when we were dead in our transgressions, [God] made us alive together with Christ (by grace you have been saved), and raised us up with Him, and seated us with Him in the heavenly places in Christ Jesus, so that in the ages to come He might show the surpassing riches of His grace in kindness toward us in Christ Jesus."

6. Gentleness

Philippians 4:5 "Let your gentle Spirit be known to all men. The Lord is near."

7. Self-control

Second Peter 1:5-8 "in your faith supply moral excellence, and in your moral excellence, knowledge, and in your knowledge, self-control, and in your self-control, perseverance, and in your perseverance, godliness, and in your godliness, brotherly kindness, and in your brotherly kindness, love. For if these qualities are yours and are increasing, they render you neither useless nor unfruitful in the true knowledge our Lord Jesus Christ."

If you read these verses and feel that you're lacking in this fruit, remember that as you trust in God, it is He who will grow this fruit in you.

God's word is key

Knowing the word of God through the power of the Holy Spirit is a key to sanctification. This should be an incentive to read and study the Bible, asking the Spirit to open your eyes to His truth. Also, understanding that God's word transforms your mind should be another reason to turn to the Bible.

Psalm 119 speaks of statutes, law, instruction, testimonies, precepts, commandments, judgments, decisions, promises, and other words which are all synonym words for the word of God, the Bible. When you read Psalm 119, you can replace these synonyms with "the word of God," so you can understand the power of God's word clearly.

Incentive to read the word of God

Psalm 119 says that by the Word of God you can have the following results after reading it:

Be blessed. Psalm 119:1-2 says you will be blessed by the word.

Prevent sin. Psalm 119:3 says you will do no iniquity and will walk in His way when you internalize the word, and verse 101 says the word keeps you from evil.

Taste. Psalm 119:103 says the word is sweeter than honey. In Bible days, honey was the best delicacy, which makes the Bible an even sweeter delicacy.

Rejoice. Psalm 119:14, 105, 111, 162 says that the word causes rejoicing.

Delight. Psalm 119:16, 35, 70, 77, 143, 174 say that the word brings delight.

Experience wonder. Psalm 119:129 says the word is wonderful.

Hope. Psalm 119:79 says the word is hope.

Experience purity. Psalm 119:140 says the word is pure.

Experience peace. Psalm 119:165 says the word is peace.

Praise. Psalm 119:171, 175 says the word is praise.

Know truth. Psalm 119:142, 160 says the word is truth.

Experience longing for the word. Psalm 119:20, 131 says your soul will long for the word of God.

Be strong. Psalm 119:28 says the word strengthens.

Experience merciful kindness and tender mercies. Psalm 119:76-77 says the word gives merciful kindness and tender mercies.

Grow in understanding. Psalm 119:27, 104, 130, 144 says the word gives so much understanding that you will desire to talk of God's wondrous works.

Experience no shame. Psalm 119:6, 116 says the word causes no shame.

Have something that is better than gold and silver. Psalm 119:72, 127 says the word is better than thousands of silver and gold.

Results from the word of God

Psalm 119 says the word of God will provide the following results:

Enlarge your heart. Psalm 119:32 says the word enlarges your heart, causing you to run to the Bible.

Help you give thanks at midnight. Psalm 119:55 says the word after being read will come to your mind at midnight; verse 62 says you will give thanks at midnight. I can say from experience this works as a result of studying the Bible.

Help you meditate. Psalm 119:97, 113 says that the word causes meditation.

Help you see good. Psalm 119:71 says the word causes you to see good in affliction; thus, God works all things together for good, as Romans 8:28 concludes.

Help you be wise. Psalm 119:98-100 says the word makes you wiser.

No fear due to the word of God

Psalm 119 says the Word will do the following for you:

Cause God's face to shine. Psalm 119:135 says that the word causes God's face to shine on you.

Be a hiding place and shield. Psalm 119:114 says that the word is your hiding place and shield.

Be a lamp and light to your feet. Psalm 119:114 says the word will be a lamp to your feet and a light for your path of walking wholeheartedly with God.

Simply understanding all that Psalm 119 says about the written word is enough incentive to keep reading and studying it, but Revelation 19:13 explodes a hunger and thirst for knowing the Living Word. It says, referring to Jesus, "He is clothed with a robe dipped in blood, and His name is called The Word of God."

The Living Word is Jesus Christ, the Savior of the world, and He is the one who uses His written word powerfully to transform our hearts and minds to help us be more like Him.

An analogy that I like to use to help people endure the stresses and trials during this sanctification process is this: God is molding and shaping us to fit into a Jesus super-suit that doesn't fit just yet. It most likely will take a lifetime, so while you wait, lean on God's understanding. Waiting and trusting and living by faith while God molds us will develop a life of love, joy, peace, patience, kindness, gentleness, and self-control. We will never achieve a life of no stress while on earth in our human bodies, but you can press on in God's word while developing relationships with likeminded Christians who can walk beside you and share with you during stresses. You might be surprised how God can use you to bless others through your past trials.

I went through an excruciating heartache in an unfaithful marriage, only to find that God has brought me to many other women who needed to hear that they were not alone in their heartaches. As God is sanctifying us and transforming our minds through His word, He will use us to encourage and help others along the way.

 ## Applications

1. According to Romans 12:2, quoted at the beginning of this chapter, what do you glean about leaning on your own understanding versus leaning on God's understanding? What does it say to do to your mind?

2. According to the Atonement section of this chapter, can we atone for our own sins? Who provides atonement?

3. According to Romans 11:26-27 in the Atonement and Covenant section, what was the covenant God made with Jacob (the Israelites and followers)?

4. According to John 17:17, what sanctifies believers?

5. According to 1 John 2:5 in the fruit of the Spirit section of this chapter, how is the love of God perfected in us?

6. According to Hebrews 12:2 in the fruit of the Spirit section of this chapter, what did joy for us cause Jesus to do?

7. According to Psalm 119:133, what should a prayer request for God be that will help us avoid sin?

 ## Actions

Make appointment

Make an appointment with God every day to read or listen to the Bible. Soak up His word so that it can transform and renew your mind.

Memorize fruit of the Spirit

Memorize the fruit of the Spirit in Galatians 5:22-23. "But the fruit of the Spirit is love, joy, peace, patience, kindness, goodness, faithfulness, gentleness, self-control; against such things there is no law."

Psalm 119

Study Psalm 119 to see all the transforming abilities of the word of God. Use the "God's word is key" section in this chapter as your guide.

CHAPTER 16

Total Trust

Daniel 3:28
Nebuchadnezzar responded and said,
"Blessed be the God of Shadrach, Meshach,
and Abed-nego,
who has sent His angel and delivered His servants
who put their trust in Him,
violating the king's command,
and yielded their bodies so as not
to serve or worship any god except their own God."

As the prophet Daniel followed God more intimately, he learned to trust God more.

When the pagan nation of Babylon conquered Judah, Nebuchadnezzar wanted some of the better youths of Israel to come to Babylon to serve him.

One of those chosen for the king's court was Daniel. He and the other young men were described as having "no defect, who were good-looking, showing intelligence in every branch of wisdom, endowed with understanding and discerning knowledge, and who had ability for serving in the king's court." (Daniel 1:4)

Can you imagine being in Daniel's place, whose home had been ripped out from under him? How could he lean on God's understanding and not be filled with fear? It could only be by the power of God. Daniel seemed to have total trust in God every step of his life. He is one of the most excellent examples of a trusting person, and there is so much to learn from reading about his life.

Daniel's determination

He refused the king's food

Upon arriving in Babylon, Daniel and his friends were served the king's meat and wine. Knowing God's law, Daniel asked the commander of the officials to allow him to refrain from food and drink sacrificed to idols but instead to have vegetables and water. It took total trust in God to approach the commander with this request. Daniel and his friends could have died for refusing orders, but God gave them special favor for their obedience. After ten days of eating vegetables and water, Daniel and his friends looked healthier than the others.

After seeing their sturdy appearance, the Babylonian officials noticed that there was something special about these young Israelite men. Of course, it was their God!

He interpreted the king's dream

God gave Daniel and his friends excellent knowledge, intelligence in literature, and wisdom. To Daniel God gave the ability to understand visions and dreams, which was a highly-prized ability in Babylon.

God's plan in giving Daniel this gift was to win the heart of the king of Babylon. When King Nebuchadnezzar had a disturbing dream, he threatened to kill all the advisors because nobody could tell him his dream and then interpret it.

But Daniel was not only able to tell the king his dream, he also gave the interpretation, so the king spared the lives of all the advisors.

Nebuchadnezzar recognized the God of Israel with praise by saying in Daniel 2:47-49, "Truly your God is the God of gods, the Lord of kings, and a revealer of secrets since you could reveal this secret." The King was so overwhelmed with God's power that he promoted Daniel, gave him many great gifts, and made him ruler and chief administrator over all the wise men of Babylon.

Daniel was able to maintain total trust in God because, instead of leaning on his own understanding, he recognized God's hand in all circumstances.

He refused to bow to King Darius

After the Persians conquered the Babylonians, Daniel served under King Darius, who greatly respected him. But the governors under the king hated this Jew, so they tricked the king into making a decree that would force everyone to bow to King Darius alone. Of course, Daniel would never agree to that decree, for he worshipped only the God of Israel.

Daniel's punishment for not worshiping Darius meant that he would be thrown into a den of lions. King Darius was devastated. In Daniel 6:16b, he said to Daniel, "Your God whom you constantly serve will Himself deliver you."

Isn't it amazing to think that Daniel could have that kind of influence over a pagan king who worshiped idols? King Darius had been so influenced by Daniel's trusting heart that he fasted and prayed to Daniel's God all night.

The next day the king showed up at the lion's den and said in verse 20, "Daniel, servant of the living God, has your God, whom you serve continually, been able to deliver you from the lions?"

Once he saw that Daniel was safe, he praised the true God, and decided to "make a decree that in all the dominion of my kingdom, men are to fear and tremble before the God of Daniel; For He is the living God, and enduring forever, And His kingdom is the one which will not be destroyed, and His dominion will be forever. He delivers and rescues and performs signs and wonders In heaven and on earth, Who has also delivered Daniel from the power of the lions." The passage goes on to say, "So this Daniel enjoyed success in the reign of Darius and in the reign of Cyrus the Persian." (Daniel 6:26-28)

Interestingly, King Cyrus, the next king of Persia after Darius, sent the governor of Jerusalem back to rebuild the temple of God. Daniel's influence of total trust in God may have contributed to the heart of Cyrus being open to God's command. Not only did Cyrus order the temple to be rebuilt, but he provided all the supplies and money for the trip and task of rebuilding.

This reaction of a pagan king reminds us that God is totally worth trusting. Learn to lean on His understanding, which will provide a life of confidence. There may be stressful things happening around you, but your reaction does not have to be one of anxiety if you trust in God's protection and provision.

Daniel's total trust

Daniel gained many qualities through God's direction that allowed him to trust totally. Following, you will see a list of some of the chapters of this book and how Daniel had these qualities that you are encouraged to develop.

Trusting through great trial (chapter 1)

In Daniel 6, Daniel believed in God, and that belief saved his life from the mouth of the lions. Maybe it took a trial this great for Daniel to believe the visions he later received about future events. These visions were so shocking that it could be that Daniel had to go through many trials to understand them.

God is the same in dealing with us. He wants to reveal His will to us, and many times it takes a test for us to see His ways. Don't panic when tests and trials are thrown your way, but ask God to teach you. James 1:2 says, "Consider it all joy, my brethren, when you encounter various trials." Remember these words when you feel stress and trials that make you feel like giving up on walking with God.

Asking for forgiveness (chapter 4)

Daniel was not a sinful man by reputation, but he was humble enough in his prayers to confess that he sinned along with his nation of Israel. Daniel 9:4-7a says, "I prayed to the Lord my God and confessed and said, 'Alas, O Lord, the great and awesome God, who keeps His covenant and lovingkindness for those who love Him and keep his commandments, we have sinned, committed iniquity, acted wickedly, and rebelled, even turning aside from Your commandments and ordinances. Moreover, we have not listened to Your servants the prophets, who spoke in Your name to our kings, our princes, our fathers, and all the people of the land. Righteousness belongs to You, O Lord, but to us open shame.'"

This confusion Daniel referred to is what sin causes. When the Israelites were in sin, they wandered, just the way they did in the wilderness for 40 years before they finally came to the Promised Land. If you're in confusion and not feeling like God is near to you, consider whether you might need to confess sin in your life or sins of others you're associated with.

Once you confess all sin, then trusting God becomes more natural, as it was for Daniel.

Listening (chapter 5)

When you walk with someone in relationship, it's important to listen to them so the relationship can grow. Daniel prayed three times a day, but he also read the word of God, which is listening to God. Daniel 9:13 shows evidence of Daniel's masterful knowledge of God's word: "As it is written in the law of Moses, all this calamity has come on us; yet we have not sought the favor of the Lord our God by turning from our iniquity and giving attention to Your truth."

Daniel knew the scriptures that he had at that time, and from them he knew there would be deliverance from captivity. He knew God so well that he understood God's heart and character enough to trust every step He laid out for him to take.

You can know God too, through listening to and reading His word daily so that you will recognize the voice of your Shepherd.

Wisdom (chapter 6)

In the hot iron story in Chapter 6, the young boy was told that the iron was hot. Once he touched the hot iron, he understood what "hot" meant, and then he had the wisdom not to touch it again.

Similarly, Daniel gained knowledge of God from reading the scriptures, knowing every detail of the lives of his ancestors, the book of Isaiah which was uncovered in the temple rubble, and words that Jeremiah had prophesied in Jerusalem during his day. This knowledge gave him an understanding of God's will for his people. After gaining the knowledge of God, he understood the truth, and God gave him extraordinary wisdom to do His will in Babylon.

Daniel 6:3b says, "he [Daniel] possessed an extraordinary spirit, and the king planned to appoint him over the entire kingdom." Throughout Daniel's life, his wisdom was on display as a gift from God.

God gives the gift of wisdom today also. If we gain knowledge through the Bible and begin to understand God's heart, He will provide us with the wisdom to do His will.

Laying it down (chapter 7)

Throughout his time in Babylon, when Daniel prayed for the city of Jerusalem where God's presence used to be, he looked towards that city. After the 70-year time frame of captivity was complete, Daniel laid down his life in prayer to be used by God to ensure God's will be done in Jerusalem as prophesied. In Daniel 9:3, he said, "So I gave my attention to the Lord God to seek Him by prayer and supplications, with fasting, sackcloth, and ashes."

God promised that His people could return to Jerusalem after 70 years, so Daniel laid down his requests, begging God to restore the territory once again. He asked on behalf of the people day in and day out.

Do you find yourself seeking God in prayer? Do you ask God for things in your life that are of eternal value? Jesus said in Matthew 7:7, "Ask, and it will be given to you; seek, and you will find." As you ask, remember to ask for God's wisdom that will help you ask according to His will.

Waiting (chapter 8)

Daniel found out that waiting on God's direction in his life could bring favor.

Daniel was anxiously awaiting and praying for the day when his people would be delivered back to their home in Jerusalem according to God's promise. In the meantime, Daniel received a new revelation of end-times events. In Daniel 12:9 the angel Gabriel said, "Go your way, Daniel, for these words are concealed and sealed up until the end of time. Many will be purged, purified, and refined, but the wicked will act wickedly; and none of the wicked will understand, but those who have insight will understand."

Daniel was thankful for the gift of wisdom and felt honored to receive the words and plans of the end times. These gifts from God made Daniel's waiting moments more bearable.

Trust in the face of enemy attack (chapter 9)

When Daniel received the prophecy from Gabriel, he found out that even God's angel had to endure a fierce enemy attack for 21 days, resulting in his having to ask the archangel Michael to help him deliver the message to Daniel.

This raging battle in the spirit realm helped put Daniel's past struggles, like the lion's den, in perspective.

This revelation of end-times events became the primary purpose of God's will for Daniel. Daniel 10:10-14 says, "Then behold, a hand touched me and set me trembling on my hands and knees. He said to me, 'O Daniel, man of high esteem, understand the words that I am about to tell you and stand upright, for I have now been sent to you.' And when he had spoken this word to me, I stood up trembling. Then he said to me, 'Do not be afraid, Daniel, for from the first day that you set your heart on understanding this and on humbling yourself before your God, your words were heard, and I have come in response to your words. But the prince of the kingdom of Persia was withstanding me for twenty-one days; then behold, Michael, one of the chief princes, came to help me, for I had been left there with the kings of Persia. Now I have come to give you an understanding of what will happen to your people in the latter days, for the vision pertains to the days yet future.'"

What an honor to serve such a powerful God! It would give Daniel more incentive to lean on God's understanding.

With all your stresses and problems in your life today, do you ever feel like you're experiencing a lion's den or maybe a battle with Satan like Gabriel? Remember that there are battles going on in the spirit realm, but God is the ultimate Victor. This will help you keep your situation in perspective.

Crying out to God (chapter 10)

When Daniel was in the lion's den, we can imagine him crying out to God for help, but how amazing that he displayed such trust while sitting with lions!

Once he heard about the king's decree in Daniel 6:10, we can see he continued to give God all glory and honor praying three times a day. "Now when Daniel knew that the document was signed, he entered his house (now in his roof chamber he had windows open toward Jerusalem); and he continued kneeling on his knees three times a day, praying and giving thanks before his God, as he had been doing previously."

We can picture in our minds the wonderful prayers Daniel cried out to God while in with the lions. The next morning when King Darius came to check on Daniel to see if he was alive, Daniel said in Daniel 6:21-22 "O King, live forever! My

God sent His angel and shut the lion's mouths and they have not harmed me."

God is glorious and all-powerful, but He is also near to us and understands all of our needs.

Trusting even to the last straw (chapter 11)

Daniel had several "last straw" moments while in Babylonian captivity. One was when Nebuchadnezzar became full of himself after he had seemed to humble himself before God. The disappointment for Daniel must have been devastating.

Have you ever felt this way when you were discipling a fellow Christian? They seemed to be growing in their faith, but then they were pulled away. Your heart cries out for that person.

Another "last straw" moment for Daniel might have been when he was thrown to the lions. He asked God to save him, trusting in His will. But he also had grown close to King Darius and was most likely thankful to hear that Darius fasted all night hoping that he was seeking God. (Daniel 6:18) When the king arrived at the den the next morning, he was hoping God had saved Daniel. King Darius was able to see God in action.

Jesus was the same way. Even while He hung on the cross about to breathe His last, He prayed, "Father, forgive them for they know not what they do." He cried out to God, not for Himself but the sake of others, that they would trust and believe in God.

Do you trust God so much that most of your prayers are for others?

Gaining strength (chapter 12)

Daniel learned that his strength came solely from God. Every time he was stopped or blocked from doing something for God while in Babylon, God lifted him to new positions of influence and strength. Many times, Daniel felt weak before God gave him strength.

For example, Daniel received many visions of the future, the nature of which were so devastating or surreal that Daniel lost his strength and felt weak. In Daniel 10:15-18, Daniel became weak when Gabriel delivered a surreal message of future end times events. "When he had spoken to me according to these words, I turned my face toward the ground and became speechless. And behold, one who resembled a human being was touching my lips; then I opened my mouth and spoke and said to him who was standing before me, 'O my lord, as a result of the vision anguish has come upon me, and I have retained no strength. For how can such a servant of my lord talk with such as my lord? As for me, there remains no strength in me, nor has any breath been left in me.' Then this one with human appearance touched me again and strengthened me."

Hebrews 11:32-34 says, "And what more shall I say? For the time would fail me to tell of the prophets [including Daniel] who out of weakness were made strong." Always remember the source of our strength is God.

Trusting during loneliness (chapter 13)

Daniel had to leave his family and relatives to go to a foreign land where people worshipped idols. He must have felt alone in pagan Babylon while worshiping his God with just a few friends.

Once Daniel was elevated to higher positions, he had to leave his friends to go live in the palace to serve the king, which meant there were no likeminded followers of God around him. That can create loneliness, but God fills that void.

Continue to press on as you follow God wholeheartedly. His word will fill your loneliness. Carve out time daily to read His word. Put verses on index cards to study while getting ready for your day, on your commute to work, or while at your computer.

Trust leads to transformation

Daniel's faith through all of the ups and downs in his life contributed to his transformation as a follower of God.

If you don't know disappointment, then you can't appreciate the fulfillment. If you don't know what it is to be in need, then you can't truly appreciate plenty. If you haven't experienced enemy attack then you won't understand the need for strength.

We can't expect to live an entirely peaceful, stress-free life as a Christian. When disappointments and struggles happen, we can cling tighter to God, remembering James 1:3-4. "The testing of your faith produces endurance. And let endurance have its perfect result, so that you may be perfect and complete, lacking in nothing."

When we're tested like Daniel and endure in faith, we will become perfect and complete, producing the fruit of the Spirit.

Daniel had that fruit: love, joy, peace, patience, kindness, gentleness, and self-control. Learning about Daniel's life through his struggles, trials and victories reminds us how important it is for us to allow the Holy Spirit to transform us and grow the fruit of the Spirit in us also.

Applications

1. According to Deuteronomy 28:45-47, what was the result when the Israelites stopped trusting in God?

2. What incentive does 2 Samuel 22:31 give to trust in God?

3. According to Hosea 10:13, what is the result of trusting in your own way and not God's ways?

4. According to Isaiah 57:13, what happens when people get caught up trusting idols instead of God? Why is it better to trust in God?

5. What does Jeremiah 17:7 say about trusting in the Lord God?

6. In Daniel 4:34-35, what reasons did Nebuchadnezzar give to trust God after he wandered as a beast in the fields of the earth?

7. According to Daniel 6:26-27 what reasons did King Darius give to trust God after witnessing Daniel's salvation from the lion's den?

 ## Actions

Pray without ceasing

Practice praying at least 3 times per day like Daniel. This can be done anywhere you are— in the car, at work, in bed, at a park, or in your prayer place. Here are some ideas what to pray for:

Family/friends	Worries in life
Your church	God's will be done
People at work	Those in need
Your country	The lost around the world

Pray Psalm 139:23-24

> "Search me, O God, and know my heart:
> Try me, and know my anxious thoughts:
> And see if there be any hurtful way in me,
> And lead me in the everlasting way."

The way everlasting is the victory of Jesus Christ in our lives. His sacrifice as the Messiah, the King of Israel, was set forth to fulfill the New Covenant in our own hearts, and eventually the new Kingdom that will be established in the final days. This is where we will live forever with Jesus and God with no pain, no tears, no wars, no stress, and no worries. Look forward to that day when Jesus will return, and trust that He is fulfilling His covenant in you even now.

Memorize Daniel's blessing

Memorize Daniel's blessing, his praise to God in Daniel 2:20-23, that he prayed after God revealed Nebuchadnezzar's dream to him. It says, "Let the name of God be blessed forever and ever, For wisdom and power belong to Him. It is He who changes the times and epochs; He removes kings and establishes kings; He gives wisdom to wise men and knowledge to men of understanding. "It is He who reveals the profound and hidden things; He knows what is in the darkness, And the light dwells with Him. To You, O God of my fathers, I give thanks and praise, For You have given me wisdom and power; Even now You have made known to me what we requested of You, For You have made known to us the king's matter."

Ask God to give you wisdom in making trustworthy decisions in your life so that you can bless and praise God for His faithfulness in your life also.

CHAPTER 17

Victory

1 Corinthians 15:57
"but thanks be to God,
who gives us the victory
through our Lord Jesus Christ."

In sports, the highlights involve victories, but the other side of the coin is defeat. The same goes for the highlights of the story of God's Old Covenant people, the Israelites. If they followed God faithfully, they would experience victory throughout their journeys, victory over trials, victory over slavery, victory in battles, and so on.

The final victory for all of God's people is the risen Lord, Jesus Christ, who makes His kingdom in our hearts now and will set up the perfect Kingdom on earth one day.

Several victories in the Bible foreshadow the final victory of Christ.

Victory in overcoming slavery

After Joseph saved the Israelites from the famine in Egypt, all of God's people lived in Egypt for safety and comfort. As time went on and Joseph's generation died, the Egyptians forgot the close ties they had with Joseph and Israel. They enslaved the Israelites, who then cried out to God for deliverance.

After hundreds of years, God raised up Moses to be that deliverer. In bringing the victory of deliverance from slavery, God did the impossible through Moses, parting the Red Sea so the Israelites could walk through on the dry land, and sweeping away the Egyptians, bringing victory.

Exodus 14:30 says, "Thus the Lord saved Israel that day from the hand of the Egyptians." Exodus 15:1-2 adds, "Then Moses and the sons of Israel sang this song to the Lord, and said, 'I will sing to the Lord, for He is highly exalted; The horse and its rider He has hurled into the sea. The Lord is my strength and song, And He has become my salvation; This is my God, and I will praise Him; My father's God, and I will extol Him.'"

When Moses and the Israelites stood on the Egyptian side of the Red Sea, the situation seemed utterly hopeless. But they discovered that God could and would do the impossible to bring victory.

Have you experienced God parting impossible seas in your life? Maybe you faced a hopeless disease, and He pulled you through, or perhaps you had no money, and He miraculously provided. Praise God for victories in our lives.

When God's people approached the Promised Land, twelve spies were sent ahead to see what kind of conditions they would face. They came back with a report of giants in the land. Ten of the men said the situation was hopeless, but two of the men, Joshua and Caleb, said not to fear because God would make provision for victory so they could defeat the giants.

Numbers 13:27-28, 30-33a says, "Thus they told him [Moses] and said, "We went in to the land where you sent us; and it certainly does flow with milk and honey, and this is its fruit. Nevertheless, the people who live in the land are strong, and the cities are fortified and very large; and moreover, we saw the descendants of Anak there. Then Caleb quieted the people before Moses and said, 'We should by all means go up and take possession of it, for we will surely overcome it.' But the men who had gone up with him said, 'We are not able to go up against the people, for they are too strong for us.' So they gave out to the sons of Israel a bad report of the land which they had spied out, saying, 'The land through which we have gone, in spying it out, is a land that devours its inhabitants; and all the people whom we saw in it are men of great size.'"

But Joshua and Caleb insisted that these giants were not a threat in the presence of God's people.

God delivered Joshua and Caleb safely as He had promised. God does fulfill His promises of victory so that we stay active in our faith and learn to trust Him more.

Victory in fighting the giant

Perhaps the most fantastic physical victory of the Bible was David's fight with Goliath, the Philistine giant.

The most remarkable fact about this battle was that David was only a young boy at that time. Of his seven brothers, only the three oldest were away at battle, which means that three others, who were still at home, must have been under 20 years of age. David was the youngest, which means that he was probably only about 14 years old at most.

How could such a young boy fight a giant?

When David took food to his older three brothers, he was appalled that the army of Israel was at a standstill and shaking in their boots.

He kept pointing out to them that God would fight this battle, even saying, "For who is this uncircumcised Philistine, that he should taunt the armies of the living God?" (1 Samuel 17:26b)

But all the other soldiers were too intimidated to even think of fighting this giant.

Finally David decided that he would fight Goliath himself. First Samuel 17:45-46a says, "Then David said to the Philistine, 'You come to me with a sword, a spear, and a javelin, but I come to you in the name of the Lord of hosts, the God of the armies of Israel, whom you have taunted. This day the Lord will deliver you up in to my hands, and I will strike you down and remove your head from you.'"

And David won that battle. David was not only successful at defeating Goliath, but he needed only one stone in his sling to finish the job.

David's trust in God was incredible. God had shown David victories while fighting wild animals as he shepherded the sheep, which gave him confidence that God would deliver this giant into his hand also.

All of the time alone with God while he tended the sheep had grown his faith and trust.

Do you spend time alone with God? Will you carve out time to be still before God like David did?

As you trust Him and follow Him, God promises to be faithful to you so that you can live a life of faithfulness to Him. You can experience His victories in your life, as David did.

Victory in rebuilding the temple

When Solomon built the temple, there were days of celebrations with musical instruments as an act of worship to the Lord. The Israelites demonstrated victory and sang songs about the deliverance God had given them from many enemies.

Hundreds of years later, when a new generation of Israelites rebuilt God's temple, this was an enormous victory too, because they had been in captivity in the pagan land of Babylon for 70 years. Finally, they could worship God in peace and have His presence in their midst.

The book of Ezra talks about the hope of new celebrations in the temple. After the temple rebuilding began, Ezra 3:11 says, "They sang, praising and giving thanks to the Lord. Saying, 'For He is good, for His lovingkindness is upon Israel forever.' And all the people shouted with a great shout when they praised the Lord because the foundation of the house of the Lord was laid."

Do you have a foundation built in your faith? Are you experiencing celebration knowing that you have eternal life when you die? Pray that God will bring you victory in the peace of worship.

Victory At Jesus' birth

Mary, who was to be the mother of Jesus, was visited by the angel Gabriel. He victoriously told her the news that as a virgin she would conceive a child by the Holy Spirit of God. The victory in this message was that the child would be the Savior of the world, the Messiah.

In Luke 1:46-49 Mary proclaimed, "My soul exalts the Lord, And my spirit has rejoiced in God my Savior. For He has had regard for the humble state of His bondslave; For behold, from this time on all generations will call me blessed. For the Mighty One has done great things for me; And Holy is His name."

Elizabeth, Mary's cousin, who was past childbearing years, conceived a son who was appointed to pave the way for the Messiah's victorious entrance to His 3½ year ministry. Gabriel told Mary that her cousin was with child, saying, "for with God, nothing will be impossible."

Do you believe that nothing is impossible with God? If not, then you are not experiencing a life knowing the victories of God.

Zacharias, Elizabeth's husband, was visited by an angel who announced news that his barren wife would conceive. Since Elizabeth was past childbearing years, Zacharias didn't believe the victorious news and became mute for nine months.

Can you pray for an open mind and faith to absorb all of the victories of God and live by them?

The world's definition of a victorious life is "lifestyles of the rich and famous," but God's definition is very different. Stay in His word and gain knowledge and understanding of it to embrace His victory.

Victory At Jesus' death

Crucifixion

Jesus' death on the cross seemed like defeat, but His crucifixion was really the beginning of the greatest victory the world has ever known.

One might think the victory of Jesus' walk on earth was His miracles: making wine from water at the wedding feast, healing people, giving sight to the blind, purging out demons, and causing lame men to walk.

These were all crucial moments in Jesus' ministry to prove that He was indeed God in the flesh, but He came to earth to defeat sin and death, to make way for us to have our sins forgiven. He was the only One who could forgive sins, because He was the perfect Lamb of God for sacrifice.

Have you embraced this forgiveness and experienced the victory of Jesus Christ?

Resurrection

After Jesus' death, He was buried and then resurrected from the dead three days later. His resurrection accomplished the victory over the hold of death. His linen cloths used in the burial were left neatly folded on the bench, and the angels stood at the entrance to the tomb. The symbolism of the folded cloths was the message, "I'm coming back."

Jesus would continue to proclaim His victory of resurrection by appearing to over 500 people at once and preparing His followers for the promised helper, the Holy Spirit. The Holy Spirit would give them victory and the power to follow God's will on earth.

Do you acknowledge the victory of Jesus' resurrection from the dead?

Victory over Satan

The battle with Satan that we must endure will come to an end during the revelation of the final days. The defeat of this battle with Satan is a huge victory and something that should give us hope as we await the return of Jesus Christ.

Revelation 12:9-10 unveils the news that Satan and his angels are cast out, bringing final victory over Satan which was prophesied at the beginning of time in Genesis 3 through Jesus' sacrifice for sin and death. Revelation 12:10 says, "Then I heard a loud voice in heaven saying, 'Now the salvation and the power and the kingdom of our God and the authority of His Christ have come, for the accuser of our brethren has been thrown down, he who accuses them before God day and night.'" Satan accuses us before God, and that will come to an end.

When we read Revelation 12, we can rejoice in the good news of victory that all of Satan's accusing will end. Revelation 12:11a continues, "And they overcame him [Satan] by the blood of the Lamb, and by the word of their testimony."

Jesus had predicted Satan's defeat throughout the Bible. John 16:11b says, "The ruler of this world (Satan) has been judged."

Praise God that He has victory over our enemy, the devil.

Victory at Jesus' return

In Revelation 2:12, the church in Pergamos received a warning letter that described Jesus as One having a two-edged sword. It is a victory sword that we possess once we receive Christ as our Lord and Savior.

In these letters, Jesus announced Himself to the different churches, to warn them to follow diligently in their walk with God. The temptation then and today is to waver in our faith and not follow God wholeheartedly.

The best way to maintain the close fellowship God desires is to read His word daily. The word is the sword according to Hebrews 4:12. "For the word of God is living and active and sharper than any two-edged sword, and piercing as far as the division of soul and spirit, of both joints and marrow, and able to judge the thoughts and intentions of the heart."

The temptation is to stop sharpening your sword daily through God's word. Avoiding God's word can cause you to become apathetic and weary of pressing on to the victorious finish line: Christ's return to set up His new Kingdom.

Revelation 2:17 presents some details of our victory through Christ: "To him who overcomes, to him I will give some of the hidden manna, and I will give him a white stone, and a new name written on the stone which no one knows but he who receives it."

God has many victorious promises for us if we will continue to follow Him wholeheartedly. Before the new heaven and new earth are established, Revelation shows us that Jesus will fight for us to make sure our future is secure. Revelation 17:14 says, "These will wage war against the Lamb, and the Lamb will overcome them, because He is Lord of lords and King of kings, and those who are with Him are the called and chosen and faithful."

Will you commit to staying faithful in your walk with Christ? Will you lean on His understanding and not your own understanding? Press on in faith and do the Actions in this book. As you trust and obey, you can experience victory in your faith.

Victory in faith

God wants believers to have victory in their faith by the sacrifice of Jesus Christ that grants eternal life. First John 5:4 says, "For whatever is born of God overcomes the world; and this is the victory that has overcome the world—our faith."

As you walk in faith, leaning on God's understanding, the Prince of this world, Satan, will continually try to deceive you. First John 2:24-26 sums up essential truths. "As for you, let that abide in you which you heard from the beginning. If what you heard from the beginning abides in you, you also will abide in the Son and in the Father. This is the promise which He Himself made to us: eternal life. These things I have written to you concerning those who are trying to deceive you."

This scripture is to warn and prepare us to follow God purely and faithfully, not allowing the world, our own desires, or the devil, to get in our way to block us. I'm sure we'd all like to hear God say to us as He did in Matthew 25:21, (NKJV) "Well done, good and faithful servant; you were faithful over a few things, I will make you ruler over many things. Enter into the joy of your Lord."

Claim Christ's victory

Transfer wandering thoughts to prayer

If you're feeling temptation and having wandering thoughts, transfer those sinful thoughts, and pray for the person or stress that occupies your mind. These prayers reach God's throne as incense and are placed in bowls of prayers of the saints.

Revelation 5:8 says, "And when he had taken the scroll, the four living creatures and the twenty-four elders fell down before the Lamb, each holding a harp, and golden bowls full of incense, which are the prayers of the saints."

What a beautiful incentive to pray all your concerns to God, since He saves them at His throne. What a victory!

Don't believe Satan's accusations

Satan accuses us and tries to bring us down daily. He whispers and sometimes screams in your ears all day every day, telling you lies, like maybe God doesn't care about you, you're not worthy of love, or God doesn't care about how you live. Satan knows he is ultimately defeated, so he doesn't want us to have the victory but wants us to suffer with him. Causing us to disobey God brings delight to Satan.

Satan also tries to make us feel hopeless by claiming that God's promises won't come about on earth.

Do you believe these lies? Jesus said to watch and wait for His return when He sets up His new Kingdom: another paradise like in the garden with the tree of life.

Satan repeats in our ears day after day that God's promises are not true. When we believe his lies, we turn to ourselves or others for help, or else we live in fear and confusion. We no longer lean on God's understanding.

There was a time in my own life when things got so hopeless that I didn't follow God as closely as I should have: not visiting my prayer place as much and not opening my Bible even to read. It was a very dark time for me because I began to want to follow the world's very empty understanding.

But eventually I resumed prayer times daily and reading and studying the Bible. After some time, I began to understand how to lean on God's understanding and trust only Him.

That hopeless time caused me to long for God and follow Him wholeheartedly and seek His will for my life more than ever. I could see that the barren time I experienced eventually helped me become stronger in my faith.

My prayer is that you will also live out the life God wants for you—one of trusting in Him wholeheartedly.

There will still be stresses and struggles from time to time, but if you stop to ask, "God, what do You want to teach me through this trial?" then you'll eventually find that you can be full of His fruit, which includes joy, peace, patience, kindness, gentleness, and self-control.

Don't give up when you face hopeless situations like those that several of my friends have faced lately. Maybe you can relate to their stories:

"Deborah" was a single mom in financial stress because of her kids' pressing issues: a car wreck, colon surgery, and glaucoma. Tragic events like these are a pile of stress thrown on a single mom who struggles paycheck to paycheck.

"Lisa" had experienced two failed marriages with men who devalued her. She got to the point that she hated the way she looked. Satan works his lies through relationship trauma like these, so never believe his lies. God values you.

"Shirley" had a hip replacement. After weeks of recovery with no relief from the pain, it was found she had a fracture next to the implant. She went through more surgery, only to find that the medicines aggravated her celiac disease. Other complications also arose, until Shirley's body reached a point of such disarray that she could hardly function to move each day. Depression set in, and she felt like giving up on her faith in God.

But when I reminded Shirley of the victory in Christ, she began to reflect on how blessed she was to know God and His word. She was blessed to have experienced fabulous works of victory through her salvation and provision for eternal life. I reminded her to dive into the word of God for encouragement and to keep believing that God can do the impossible. Shirley thanked me and has grown in the sweetness of her faith in spite of her pain. Every day she recovers a little more.

The kind of stress in these examples, and maybe your case, can be overwhelming. You might want to give up on God and lean on the world, to respond the way they would respond, imbibing their false philosophies or self-medicating to try to deaden the pain.

But God wants us to turn to Him for relief by leaning on His understanding. God's word will give us examples of victories amid stress. Look in the word to see that most victory cannot occur without a struggle. No war can be won without a battle.

One verse that can give us hope during these stresses and trials is 1 Corinthians 10:13. "No temptation has overtaken you but such as is common to man, and God is faithful, who will not allow you to be tempted beyond what you are able, but with the temptation will provide the way of escape also, so that you may be able to endure it."

Stick close to Jesus Christ as you learn to lean on God's understanding.

 Applications

1. What defeat did Jonah face in Jonah 1:1-3 and 17?

2. According to Jonah 2:10; 3:5, what was the victory of God?

3. In Luke 24:15-17, what expression of defeat did two of Jesus' followers show as they walked on the road to Emmaus? (See verse 17.)

4. According to Luke 24:30-35, what did these followers of Christ do to encourage other followers?

5. What defeat is in your life that God wants to turn into victory?

6. What if God's answer to this defeat is not what you think it should be? Will you trust in Him?

7. According to some of the previous Actions in this book, how will you commit to have victory of hope and faith in God? Describe how some of these have helped you.

 Actions

Memorize and quote verses

Every morning upon awakening, flood your mind with verses to praise God and glorify Him. Remember the victory He has provided for you through Christ to gain eternal life.

Psalm 118:24 "This is the day which the Lord has made; Let us rejoice and be glad in it."

Psalm 5:3 "In the morning, O Lord, You will hear my voice; In the morning I will order my prayer to You and eagerly watch."

Psalm 55:17 (NKJV) "Evening and morning and at noon I will pray, and cry aloud, and He shall hear my voice."

Psalm 88:13 "But I, O Lord, have cried out to You for help, And in the morning my prayer comes before You."

Psalm 92:1-2 "It is good to give thanks to the Lord and to sing praises to Your name, O Most High; To declare Your lovingkindness in the morning and Your faithfulness by night."

At night when you go to bed, you can leave your cell phone in another room and turn off the television. This way you can praise God for His victory and glory upon going to bed at night and upon rising in the morning.

Make sure to give God all of the glory in life. The world, and our own flesh, will say "don't shut me out" and "praise me," but God says to shut out the world and lean on His understanding and give Him the praise. This way you will always recognize the victory in Christ and do His will while glorifying Him.

CHAPTER 18

Look to the Prize

1 Corinthians 9:24-25 (NKJV)
"Do you not know that those who run in a race
all run, but one receives the prize?
Run In such a way that you may obtain it.
And everyone who competes for the prize
is temperate in all things.
Now they do it to obtain a perishable crown,
but we for an imperishable crown."

The apostle Paul spoke about getting a crown in heaven, which is the prize each faithful Christian gains while on earth. First Thessalonians 2:19 tells us the crown is the people each Christian has led to saving faith in Christ. "For who is our hope or joy or crown of exultation? Is it not even you, in the presence of our Lord Jesus at His coming?"

Jesus' final commission to His disciples was to make disciples of all nations. Those disciples were then in turn to make other disciples—more Christians who joyfully follow Christ.

Jesus told a parable about a shepherd leaving the 99 sheep to save the one lost sheep. Leading people to Christ through the gospel message is a glorious outflow of the work God has done in our own hearts.

Does the thought of sharing the good news of Christ scare you to death? Many people would say yes. How can we overcome our fear of doing God's will? This chapter explores the prize in the Bible to uncover the answers to this question.

Jesus' prize: lost souls

Throughout the three years of Jesus' ministry, He made it evident again and again that the prize He pursued was the lost souls of all humanity. Luke 23 shows a picture of Jesus' goal to gain His prize.

He was willing to be falsely accused

The prize Jesus desired when He came to earth and died for the sins of man, came with many obstacles. For instance, when He was on trial and handed over to Pontius Pilate, the Roman governor of Judah, He was falsely accused of treason for claiming that He was a king. Luke 23:2 says, "We found this man misleading our nation and forbidding to pay taxes to Caesar, and saying that He Himself is Christ, a King."

Jesus' kingdom was not of this world, so Pilate didn't have to worry about a rival to Caesar's throne. But Jesus endured this false accusation in order to get to the goal of giving His life as a sacrifice—that way He would gain the prize of eternal life for all who would believe in Him.

When Jesus was accused, He always stayed calm. When Pilate asked, "Are you the King of the Jews?" Jesus answered him simply and calmly, saying, "It is as you say." (Luke 23:3)

Jesus kept His eyes fixed on the prize: our lost souls who needed a blood sacrifice that only His blood could remedy.

Praise God that He stayed confident with calm answers. If He had put up a defense, they might have set Him free, which means He wouldn't have died for our sins.

Pilate found no fault with Jesus, but the people demanded in Luke 23:18, "Away with this man, and release for us [the thief and murderer] Barabbas."

Jesus was unjustly charged, but His reaction was calm, showing no emotion. His goal was to go to the cross to die for all, including these accusers. He wanted to allow them, and all of us, to have the opportunity for salvation and eternal life.

He was willing to be mocked

Leaders and soldiers also mocked Jesus as He was passed around from courtroom to courtroom as He approached the cross of Calvary. Luke 23:8 says, "Now Herod was very glad when he saw Jesus; for he had wanted to see Him for a long time, because he had been hearing about Him and was hoping to see some sign performed by Him."

When Herod questioned Jesus and got no answer, "after treating Him with contempt and mocking Him, [he] dressed Him in a gorgeous robe and sent Him back to Pilate." (Luke 23:11)

Why would Jesus tolerate this type of treatment? It was the prize that He was focused on, and not Himself.

Do you find yourself being self-focused and not looking to God's will for humanity? His desire is for the lost souls to be saved. Can you join in and help?

The prize For Jesus' disciples

Next, in John 20, another picture of Jesus' goal and prize is revealed.

The prize of Jesus' resurrection

After Jesus died and was buried, His disciples lost hope and felt defeated.

But when Peter came to the tomb to find the stone rolled away, no body in the tomb, and the cloth from Jesus' face neatly folded, he was hopeful. Peter knew according to Jewish custom that the folded cloth meant the Master would be back soon. Peter, along with John, who was with him, believed.

John 20:6-9 says, "And so Simon Peter also came, following him, and entered the tomb; and he saw the linen wrappings lying there, and a face-cloth which had been on His head, not lying with the linen wrappings, but rolled up in a place by itself. So the other disciple who had first come to the tomb then also entered, and he saw and believed. For as yet they did not understand the Scripture, that He must rise again from the dead."

When Jesus' followers saw Him resurrected from the dead, they believed. But Thomas hadn't seen Him yet and refused to accept the messages people told him about Jesus being alive again. John 20:25-28 says, "So the other disciples were saying to him, 'We have seen the Lord!' But he said to them, 'Unless I see in His hands the imprint of the nails, and put my finger into the place of the nails, and put my hand into His side, I will not believe.' After eight days His disciples were again inside, and Thomas with them. Jesus came, the doors having been shut, and stood in their midst and said, 'Peace be with you.' Then He said to Thomas, 'Reach here with your finger, and see My hands; and reach here your hand, and put it into My side; and do not be unbelieving, but believing.' Thomas answered and said to Him, 'My Lord and my God.'"

Now Thomas could look to the prize and serve Jesus wholeheartedly to carry out God's will.

How about you? Will you pray and ask God to reveal Himself to you?

Now all the disciples believed and had confidence that Jesus would return to show them His will and what they should do for Him, and He did, dissipating all the fear and anxiety they had experienced over His death. Now their primary focus was God's will.

Now they could look to the prize of serving Jesus fully, in the power of the Holy Spirit, without fearfully running for their lives. Their extreme fear gave way to hope and peace, and they could again wholeheartedly lean on God's understanding.

The prize for the disciples and for us while delivering the gospel message to others is the resurrection of Christ.

The prize for Mary Magdalene

Mary Magdalene, a close follower of Christ, stood outside the empty tomb weeping about Jesus' missing body, because she had loved and followed Him so greatly.

The angels told her that Jesus had risen as He said He would do three days after His death. When Jesus appeared to Mary, her weeping turned to great joy.

Have you ever experienced this type of joy when someone you thought was dead returned to you? If so, then you can understand a bit of the joy Mary experienced and can imagine the great love she felt for her Lord and Savior.

Once Jesus was in her presence, her sorrow was gone and her life was transformed. That was her prize.

The prize of souls

At the end of Jesus' ministry, He gave the disciples and followers directions that we call the Great Commission, to make disciples around the world. Matthew 28:18-20 says, "And Jesus came up and spoke to them, saying, 'All authority has been given to Me in heaven and on earth. Go therefore and make disciples of all the nations, baptizing them in the name of the Father and the Son and the Holy Spirit, teaching them to observe all that I commanded you; and lo, I am with you always, even to the end of the age.'"

The truth of the resurrection would help people believe, when they were told that Jesus died for their sins and now is alive. The disciples would now work for the same prize Jesus came to gain: to win souls.

Life In Jesus' Name

Jesus revealed Himself to over 500 witnesses at once. John 20:30 says, "Therefore many other signs Jesus also performed in the presence of the disciples." These miraculous signs were performed so that all would believe that Jesus was the Messiah promised by God, risen again victorious over death.

After Jesus' disciples saw that truth clearly, they could confidently take the message of eternal life in Christ to the ends of the earth.

Everlasting life is truly the prize that we all look forward to: eternal life through Jesus' sacrifice on the cross for our sins, burial, and resurrection from the dead.

The prize for believers

Winning souls

The apostle Paul described the prize for believers when he wrote in Colossians 4:2-6, "Devote yourselves to prayer, being alert in it with an attitude of thanksgiving; praying at the same time for us as well, that God will open up to us a door for the word, so that we may speak the mystery of Christ, for which I have also been imprisoned; that I may make it clear, in the way I ought to speak. Conduct yourselves with wisdom toward outsiders, making the most of the opportunity. Let your speech always be with grace, as though seasoned with salt, so that you will know how you should respond to each person."

Paul underwent more stress for telling the good news of Christ than most people on the planet. He was kidnapped, flogged, threatened many times, ridiculed, ignored, shipwrecked, beaten almost unto death, and the list goes on. His focus was to win souls of the lost for Christ, which was Jesus' great commission for all believers.

Paul said, "However, I consider my life worth nothing to me; my only aim is to finish the race and complete the task the Lord Jesus has given me the task of testifying to the good news of God's grace." (Acts 20:24 NIV)

Having Paul's attitude about sharing the gospel would transform our focus to meeting the needs of others. In fact, this compassion for others makes it easier to lean on God's understanding.

Gaining an attitude like Paul's to share the hope of the gospel of Jesus Christ with others will give us compassion for people. I remember when I began to share my faith, how I began to pray for everyone that I met and was concerned for the future destination of others. I wanted to see people in heaven with me and wanted to make sure that they knew the truth of how to enter heaven when they died.

Pray for God to give you a heart for winning souls to Christ, which is the prize for believers. If you had fantastic news that could cure a rampant disease, wouldn't you tell many people? You would begin by telling your close circles of loved ones, then the town and later, taking it out as far as you can go.

Psalm 105:1 says, "O give thanks to the Lord, call upon His name; Make known His deeds among the peoples." He has granted eternal life to all of the lost people if they will believe, but they need to hear someone tell them the good news.

Many Christians are still afraid to share the gospel with unbelievers, but the least we can do is pray. Matthew 9:37 says, "The harvest is plentiful, but the workers are few. Therefore beseech the Lord of the harvest to send out workers into His harvest." If you're too afraid to share, then pray for the people you come into contact with, pray for God to send other Christians to them, or buy some gospel tracts at a place like www.livingwaters.com. They have some conversational tracts that grab people's attention. When I first began using these, I left them places and could see people picking them up right away.

A bonus of sharing your faith with unbelievers is that ailments like depression, sadness, worry, and stress will seem insignificant in light of the fate of the lost person.

Here are some steps to begin doing God's will of the Great Commission:

1. Pray

Write down people's name who you know who need salvation. Lay these names out at your prayer place, as described in chapter 7. Entrust them to God and ask Him to prepare conversations and times for you or someone else to share Christ with them.

Since this is God's will for every believer, He is faithful to orchestrate meetings. Once you pray about this, don't be surprised if in the hustle and bustle of shopping or work or taking your children to the playground, you find yourself sharing Christ with people God brings to you.

Don't fret about the time this takes, because you'll be surprised at how the Lord restores the hours we spend spreading His good news.

2. Show love

Show love and gentleness as you share the good news of Christ. Philippians 4:5b-7 says, "Let your gentleness be known to all men. The Lord is at hand. Be anxious for nothing but in everything by prayer and supplication with thanksgiving let your requests be made known to God. And the peace of God, which surpasses all comprehension, will guard your hearts your minds in Christ Jesus."

As you share the gospel, guard your heart and mind against fear, remembering that God will speak through you. If someone were bleeding on the side of the road, you would boldly stop to help in love. God will give you that same boldness with family members and strangers who might die without Christ.

3. Expose sin

Many people today believe that they haven't sinned at all. When the rich young ruler asked how he could have eternal life, he thought he had kept all the commandments that Jesus told him in Luke 18:20, "You know the commandments: 'Do not commit adultery, Do not murder, Do not steal, Do not bear false witness, Honor your father and your mother.'"

It's important to expose what sin is so that people understand how much they need the solution of forgiveness that Jesus offers.

4. Present the solution

Once when I was explaining the reality of sin to someone, they interrupted with the words, "What's the solution?"

When they understand that they have offended a perfect and Holy God, many people are anxious for a solution to this problem of sin.

After someone sees that they have sinned against God, you can present the solution of Christ crucified to take all their sins upon Himself, buried, and raised from the dead, to give them power over sin in their lives. This is excellent news!

Discipling new believers

The most significant prize in life is seeing someone come to faith in Jesus Christ after having had the honor of sharing the good news of Christ.

After the person has believed and accepted Christ as their Lord and Savior, they need to be discipled. If you're not able to get together with them regularly for long-term discipling, you can let them know about finding a local church, getting www.biblegateway.com, the Holy Bible app, Ashley T Lee app, and other resources to grow in God's word.

The Bride of Christ

When Jesus comes back to set up His final kingdom, He will have victory for eternity, so let's watch and wait for His return. You can embrace the victory of eternal life and look forward to this exciting time of Jesus' return to earth to set up His new Kingdom. Proverbs 8:34 says, "Blessed is the man who listens to me, Watching daily at my gates, Waiting at my doorposts."

Imagine being a parent or grandparent, leaving a legacy for your kids. What would be the most important stories to tell them? Stories about the coming of Jesus Christ for their salvation, and stories about the new heaven and earth in the new Kingdom.

Revelation 21:2b says that the holy city will be "made ready as a bride adorned for her husband [Christ]." Revelation 21 goes on to describe the city of pure gold will have twelve gates of pearl, walls of jasper, foundations adorned with precious stones, and streets of pure gold.

This will be unlike anything we have ever witnessed, and it will be part of our prize while in heaven.

There will be no tears. God promises to wipe away every tear.

There will be no death. In the new heaven and new earth there will be no death just like back in the Garden of Eden.

There will be no sorrow. What a prize that there will be no sorrow in the new Kingdom! Sadness and sorrow are so prevalent today but will be alleviated one day.

There will be no pain. Paul complained of a thorn in his flesh and asked God to remove it. Whatever it was, we know it was painful. Our pain and aches will all be removed in heaven, never to return again. What a victory!

Hold fast to the end to receive the prize waiting for you. Psalm 54:4-5 reminds us as we wait, "Behold, God is my helper; the Lord is the sustainer of my soul. He will recompense the evil to my foes; destroy them in Your faithfulness."

During the waiting for the prize, don't worry, don't fret, and don't agonize, but lean on God's understanding in order to have a worshipful, stress-free life in Christ.

Applications

1. What is a prize of coming to faith in Jesus according to Matthew 11:28?

2. Does that prize make it easier to stay focused on leaning on God's understanding? Why?

3. In order to gain the prize from God, what should we be telling Him according to Isaiah 6:8?

4. According to Proverbs 11:30, what does a wise person do?

5. According to Acts 13:47, what has God commanded us to do?

6. According to Philippians 3:14 and 20, what is the prize?

7. According to John 3:17, what did Jesus come to earth to do for the world?

Actions

Pray for the lost

Pray for people you know who are not saved. Maybe they are skeptical or do not believe in God. Write their names on your prayer sheet.

Memorize promises

Memorize promise verses from the book of Revelation. This book comes with a promise of a blessing if you read it, so memorizing will be the same blessing. This is a prize to us.

Revelation 4:8b "Holy, holy, holy is the Lord God, the Almighty, who was and who is and who is to come."

Revelation 4:11 "Worthy are You, our Lord and our God, to receive glory and honor and power; for You created all things, and because of Your will they existed, and were created."

Revelation 15:3-4 "Great and marvelous are Your works, O Lord God, the Almighty; Righteous and true are Your ways, King of the nations! Who will not fear, O Lord, and glorify Your name? For You alone are holy; For all the nations will come and worship before You, For Your righteous acts have been revealed."

About the Author

With a heart full of compassion, Ashley T Lee strives to help others develop a strong, passionate relationship with the Lord Jesus Christ in the best ways she knows: writing and speaking. Her ministry has given her opportunities to speak to women's groups and present one-minute radio segments for hundreds of Christian radio stations across the country.

Having evangelized on college campuses using Way of the Master ministries, Ashley is now pursuing her master's degree from Southern Evangelical Seminary.

In her free time, Ashley loves to spend time with her four daughters and her grandchildren. You can connect with her at ashleytlee.com.

Made in the USA
Columbia, SC
17 February 2020